How We Survived
in UHF Television

How We Survived in UHF Television

A Broadcasting Memoir, 1953–1984

KITTY BROMAN PUTNAM
and WILLIAM LOWELL PUTNAM

McFarland & Company, Inc., Publishers
Jefferson, North Carolina, and London

ALSO OF INTEREST: William Lowell Putnam has written several books for McFarland including *Great Railroad Tunnels of North America* (2011), *Percival Lowell's Big Red Car: The Tale of an Astronomer and a 1911 Stevens-Duryea* (2002), *The Kaiser's Merchant Ships in World War I* (2001), and *John Peter Zenger and the Fundamental Freedom* (1997).

All photographs used in this book represent the work product and property of Springfield Television Corporation, of which the authors were chairman and president.

Frontispiece: WLP: "Just where is Mae West, anyhow?"
KEF: "Don't I look better than her?"

LIBRARY OF CONGRESS CATALOGUING-IN-PUBLICATION DATA

Putnam, Kathryn Broman.
    How we survived in UHF television : a broadcasting memoir, 1953–1984 / Kitty Broman Putnam and William Lowell Putnam.
        p.   cm.
    Includes index.

    ISBN 978-0-7864-6666-5
    softcover : acid free paper ∞

    1. Television broadcasting — United States.   2. Television journalists — United States — Biography.   3. Putnam, William Lowell.   4. Putnam, Kathryn Broman.   I. Putnam, William Lowell.   II. Title.
HE8700.8.P88 2012
384.55'40973 — dc23   2011039670

BRITISH LIBRARY CATALOGUING DATA ARE AVAILABLE

Front cover: Kitty and William Putnam (courtesy Springfield Television Corporation); cover design by David K. Landis (Shake It Loose Graphics)

Manufactured in the United States of America

McFarland & Company, Inc., Publishers
  Box 611, Jefferson, North Carolina 28640
  www.mcfarlandpub.com

Most of our closest associates in building Springfield Television Corporation — WWLP, WKEF, and KSTU — have now gone on to a greater reward than we were able to offer.

Thus, before we, too, fade to black — we dedicate this volume of our reminiscences to the memory of Burleigh Brown, John A. Fergie, James H. Ferguson, Roland L. Filiault, Martin E. Firestone, Howard Keefe, Edward M. Kennedy, Lucian Marek, Margaret McGee, George J. Mitchell, Harry Robator, Wallace J. Sawyer, Donald C. Shaw, Keith Silver, George R. Townsend, Hermenus J. Vadnais, Kenneth M. Waite, and the many others who labored beside and for us.

The on-camera news team in 1964: Ed Hatch, Tom Colton, Rollie Jacobs and Ed Kennedy.

Table of Contents

Authors' Note	1
Preface	3
1. Getting Started in Television	9
2. Actually Building a Station	21
3. Lowering Our Frequency — Overnight	36
4. Parentheses	40
5. Building a Local Audience	50
6. Those Magnificent Irishmen	89
7. Building a Network Relationship	102
8. Building Advertiser Support	123
9. Not All Hard Work — Boys Will Be Boys	130
10. Onto the National Scene	144
11. Editorials in the "Fairness" Era	152
12. Dealing with the FCC	161
13. Building the Broadcast Industry — Kitty's Station	178
14. Glimpsing the Future	194
15. Personalities	199
16. A Poetic Heritage Comes Out	203
Appendix A	217
Appendix B	224
Index	231

Authors' Note

This is a very personal narrative, co-authored by two of the better-known names in American television broadcast station management of a generation ago — William Lowell (Bill) Putnam (an alpinist at heart, as well as the acknowledged ringleader of UHF-TV licensees) and his talented wife, Kathryn Elizabeth, known to the world of television as Kitty Broman, featured hostess of the longest-running local "cooking" show on television and the first woman elected to the National Association of Broadcasters Television Board, and then its chairman! In the days when seven was the ownership maximum, they ended up as builder/operators of three television stations, two of them NBC-TV affiliates: WWLP (Bill's initials and now owned by Lin Broadcasting) in Springfield, Massachusetts; WKEF (Kitty's maiden initials and now owned by the Sinclair Group) in Dayton, Ohio; and KSTU in Salt Lake City (now a Fox O & O station).

In their own words — some his (WLP), some hers (KBP), some mutual — they tell about how they got started, how they labored for survival during the "dozen lean years," and some of the events along their way to leadership roles in the world of advertiser-supported, free-to-the-viewer, over-the-air television. The sometimes brutally frank vignettes of their lives are largely consecutive, though by the time this opus was prepared, a good many of their memories had become compounded due to many subsequent adventures. Furthermore, while some of this has obviously been composed with a few tears of nostalgia, the authors assure the readers that it is reliably factual, if not always complimentary to everyone mentioned.

This noteworthy team is still to be found, primarily in Flagstaff, Arizona, where Bill is the sole trustee of a different type of "family" enterprise, his great-uncle Percival Lowell's astronomical observatory (home of the expanding universe, the rings of Uranus, and birthplace of the planet

1

Pluto), and Kitty's style of charm, cookery and entertaining are reaching new heights — no less than 2,200 meters (7,200 feet) above sea level — and where she continues to clean up after his verbal forays.

The alpinists of the United States have since elected Bill their honorary president, and the various descendants of this unique couple, ten grandchildren and a couple of "greats," all refer to Kitty with a deservedly special mix of awe and affection.

Kitty was born in Pittsburgh, and recently celebrated her 95th birthday. She was a frequent participant in amateur theatricals and had an extensive modeling career in Springfield before seeking a full-time job at the Greater Springfield Chamber of Commerce, where she encountered the opening in to television broadcasting. She chaired the New England Chapter of the American Women in Radio and Television and was later elected — almost unanimously — by the television broadcasters of the United States to their association board of directors.

Bill, slightly younger than his wife and a decorated veteran of the Mountain Troops in World War II, was born in Springfield, Massachusetts, and avers that he is primarily an alpinist, a talent that came in handy when beacon lightbulbs needed replacement, but he did chair the all-industry committee that led to the introduction of closed-captioning for many television productions. Within the television industry he also led the campaign for UHF parity, as well as for resuming broadcast editorials, that ultimately led to the retraction of the misnamed "Fairness Doctrine." To this day, he still says prayers for the peaceful repose of the soul of Robert Emmet Lee and continues to frequent the mountains of western Canada where he made numerous first ascents.

Preface

Our grandchildren have no knowledge of a world in which visual electronic media do not include color, animation, instant satellite relays (replays, too) and countless special effects. But broadcast television began without any such enhancements. One of Kitty's subsequent sponsors, the Forbes & Wallace Department Store, brought a traveling display of closed-circuit, black and white television to Springfield, MA, in the late 1930s, when the Federal Communications Commission was in the process of allocating space for four channels—1 through 4—prior to the outbreak of World War II. These allocations were in what was known as the Very High Frequencies (VHF), beginning at 44 MHz and ending at 68 MHz.

It is worth noting that the technology of radio waves has invariably made use of the lowest available frequencies and declared that anything higher in the Hertzian ether is unworkable. Thus, with the onset of World War II, the Armed Forces of the United States conscripted the basically unused Channel 1 (44–50 MHz) for ground troops' "walkie-talkie" purposes, because they declared that any frequency higher than that was simply unusable. One of the authors was exposed to such an apparatus during the course of that conflict, and should have retained the knowledge, for — like a lot of subsequently manufactured first-generation electronic equipment — its battery-powered hot tubes were not always reliable.

This is a tale of making use of various "unusable" frequencies, of using equipment that our grandchildren, whose tiny, solid-state cell phones and texting devices are perpetually active, as well as their mothers' hand-held Blackberries and iPhones. This is also a tale of doing many things in what is now obviously the hard way, because, back in those "olden days," there was no known or possible other way.

Today, the various cell phones and other mobile devices in such common use operate at frequencies that were declared beyond discussion as

3

"utterly impractical" as recently as when we started out in the summer of 1952 to build WWLP.

Before we proceed further, comprehension of a good part of the narrative below might be better if we offer a brief layman's synopsis of the frequency bands used for broadcasting in North America. These are all assigned by international agreements worked out in periodic World Administrative Radio Conferences (generally now held in Geneva) to which the first American representative (in 1903) was the distinguished Arctic hero, Major General Adolphus Washington Greely (1844–1935), hero, as well, of the San Francisco earthquake of 1906 and longtime chief of the U.S. Army Signal Corps. These conferences have defined the allocation of initial call letters and the broad parameters of what services should be accommodated without interference in which parts of the radio spectrum, while leaving the domestic details to be decided by each nation on its own.

Initially, the call letters N and W (and some of K) were allocated to the United States (though A and N are now reserved for governmental facilities); much of C pertains to Canada (with some to China); and much of M to Mexico; most of A originally to Austria; B to Great Britain; F to France; I to Italy; D (and some of K) to Germany (which lost the rest of K after World War I — as Austria lost A, along with its navy, merchant marine and all access to salt water).

Initially begun in order to avoid conflicts and interferences, this process of amicable (if the bitter and short-sighted Treaty of Versailles can be described by that adjective) international agreement has resulted in the worldwide use of radio waves to a degree undreamed-of by the best-known pioneers of radio usage: the Scottish professor of physics and astronomy, James Clerk Maxwell (1831–1879); the near-contemporary German experimenter with electromagnetic waves, Heinrich Rudolph Hertz (1857–1889); the Canadian physicist, Reginald Aubrey Fessenden (1866–1932), whose first audio transmissions were made in 1900; and the Italian inventor of directional antennae, Marchese Guglielmo Marconi (1874–1937).

Incidentally, Marconi started his radio experiments in Bologna in 1895, communicating by wireless with his uncle on the family farm outside of town, but his move to England the next year (his mother was Irish) became a major unsung factor in World War I. Marconi's further development of directional antennae ultimately allowed the Royal Navy to eavesdrop on all orders to and movements of the much and justly feared German High Seas Fleet. (When the two fleets finally met off the Danish peninsula of Jutland in the late spring of 1916, German gunnery and armor were so much more effective than those of the much larger British force that His Majesty's Home Fleets suffered far greater losses than those of the Germans. Nevertheless, Grand Admiral Alfred von Tirpitz lost heart in the face of overwhelming numbers and the High Seas Fleet was withdrawn as fast as possible to its home port of Kiel. Britannia — with Marconi's continued help — still ruled the waves.)

The radio spectrum is arbitrarily divided by decimal multiples of the number 3 for ease of definition. Hertz, Fessenden and Marconi used only Low Frequencies — from 30 to 300 Hz (Hertzian cycles) — which was all they could figure out how to work with. With the passage of time and the evolution of technology, higher and higher frequencies (with increasingly shorter wavelengths) have gradually become usable (the AM radio and Ham — the misnamed "short wave" — bands are in the Medium Frequencies — 300 to 3,000 KHz). By the time broadcast television (*fernsehen* to Hertz) came along, all manner of users — particularly the seaborne — had taken up residence in the High Frequencies (3 to 30 MHz). Thus, the first television channels had — by tradition — to be in what had become called the Very High Frequencies (VHF — 30 to 300 MHz), beyond which were increasingly "unuseable" wavelengths, culminating in visible light.

In due course, even that arbitrary nomenclative barrier was breached, producing the then incomprehensibly high "ethereal" space called Ultra High Frequency (UHF — 300 to 3,000 MHz). Even later there came the Super High Frequencies — above 3,000 MHz — and mankind is now using the Extremely High Frequency band. No matter what the nomenclature, user or content, longer waves, on the lower frequencies, behave more like sound and tend to bend around obstacles; shorter waves on higher frequencies behave more like light and are shadowed, refracted and reflected by and behind obstacles like mountains, trees (particularly the non-deciduous variety) and buildings. However, vastly smaller and more sensitive receivers have continued to make these — for years unbelievable — usages of radio (Hertzian) waves ever more possible.

In North America, television channels 2, 3 and 4 (each being 6 MHz in width, according to the standards developed in the 1930s by the first National Television Standards Committee) are adjacent, between 54 and 72 MHz. Channels 5 and 6 are also adjacent, but separated by four MHz — formerly the FM radio band — from Channel 4. Channels 7 through 13 (the "High" VHF-TV band) are adjacent and occupy the space from 176 to 216 MHz. This is why one does not find a Channel 2 transmitting in the same town as a Channel 3, though 2 is quite compatible with 4. Similarly, 5 and 6 cannot coexist. In the "high" VHF band, the allocations system allows for transmitters on Channels 7, 9, 11 and 13 to be co-located; those on Channels 8, 10 and 12 must be sufficiently distant from the odd numbers but are equally compatible with each other. In the UHF band, Channels 14 through 83 occupy the space between 470 and 890 MHz (though in the late 20th century the FCC allowed for sharing some of the lower and all of the top fourteen channels with land-mobile users).

Nowhere, however, can one find any terrestrial service on Channel 37; this frequency (608–614 MHz) has been reserved worldwide for scientific study, mostly by radio astronomers, because of its relationship to hydrogen, the basic building block of the universe. Incidentally, there is a vastly greater difference in frequency and hence wavelength and propagation characteristics between Channels 6 and 7 (both in the VHF band) than there is between Channels 13 and 14 (between which is that arbitrary barrier in nomenclature).

In order to avoid destructive interferences, various mileage spacings have been established between channels on the same frequency as well as those adjacent. These spacings are tighter in the more populous East than in the less densely populated South and West. Within the UHF TV band, the mileage separation requirements are slightly more complicated, in order to compensate for receiver oscillations and interferences. The FCC's Sixth Report on TV allocations, which opened up the UHF TV band, decreed that each operating channel must protect not only the co-channels and adjacent channels (both up and down) but also those which were removed by 7, 8, 14 and 15 (also both up and down).

Before we forget, besides probing the scrapbooks and memories of our children and several former employees, we are indebted to Cory Dunham, one-time chief in-house counsel to NBC; to an old friend of days in the mountains, Jim McCarthy, "Kitty's lawyer," who toned down some of Bill's more libelous comments; and to Peter Rosenthal, another dear friend whose great photographic talents were essential to revive some of our visual memories for this publication. Some of the pictures used herein are from Kitty's personal scrapbook; others were given us from the files we left behind at WWLP, where they were hidden, and thus preserved from destruction, by some of our loyal former employees.

During our thirty-plus years in the television broadcasting game, there was one person who consistently managed to ferret out the truth and inside workings of the industry's regulators and decision-makers, fair or foul, for better or for worse — the late Dawson B. "Tack" Nail, latterly of Falls Church, Virginia. We have been honored by his willingness to "fact check" this book in its manuscript stage, and it has thereby been considerably improved.

1

Getting Started in Television

[WLP] One morning in the late winter of 1961, after we'd been on the air for nearly eight years and while I was outside WWLP shoveling some snow, the PA system at the station blared out, *"Bill Putnam! Bill Putnam! Return to your office at once. The chairman of the FCC is calling!"*

As I made my way back through the building, I had to endure several guffaws—"They finally got you, Boss." "Hope there's not much jail time for you." "Watch your language with that guy." "Guess he didn't like last night's editorial." "Is the police chief on his way up, too?" "Are we all out of work, or will he settle for just you?"

When I finally reached our office, Kitty had a seriously worried look: "William! What have you done now?" I grinned at her, for I wasn't very concerned. With the election of John Fitzgerald Kennedy, there was finally an idealistic administration in Washington, as had been reflected in recent personnel changes at the top of the Federal Communications Commission. Furthermore, I also knew that by tradition when the FCC had something official to state to a licensee, particularly something that licensee might *not* want to hear, it was invariably done by telegram, and always came from its official secretary, never the chairman. This had to be special, maybe personal, and couldn't help but be good.

I took up the receiver and spoke: "Bill Putnam here; what can I do for you?"

The female voice (belonging to Gloria Coe) on the other end replied, "Mr. Putnam, Chairman Minow wants to talk with you; I'll put him right on."

This is really a narrative of survival. When we started this adventure, we both expected to work for our livings, but had no idea how difficult and narrow would be our escape from oblivion. In the early spring of 1952, when we were both employed at the Springfield (Massachusetts) Chamber of Commerce — one of us as manager of the Merchants' Bureau, the other as receptionist/secretary — a chamber member who ran a local radio station, Alan Tindal of WSPR, stopped by to ask if the chamber had any leads on sources of capital with which to start a television station, since there were soon to be some allocations available in the area, and a local TV outlet might be a good thing for the community.

We had known Alan for some time, a very decent person and one we wanted to help. Quite coincidentally, my maiden great-aunt, Elizabeth Putnam, had recently died and the trust fund set up by her father, my great-grandfather, George Putnam (1834–1912), was then in the process of distribution to its numerous ultimate beneficiaries — of which I was one — so (thinking myself adequately flush and with no intention of spending the rest of my days at the chamber) I responded to the effect that Alan didn't have to go any further; I'd be his investor. Alan thanked me and left, and Kitty and I returned to whatever we were being paid to do, while contemplating a possible future in the embryonic field of broadcast television.

In mid–1948, the FCC — in its collective wisdom — decided that television was likely becoming too popular for the 12 channels it had so far made available. So the Commission stopped issuing permits for any channel until it could find more space it deemed suitable to meet the apparent demand. Four years later the FCC officially announced that there was such space farther up in the radio spectrum and that it had evolved a plan for its use. This four-year hiatus served to perpetuate the 108 existing VHF outlets as quasi-monopolistic franchises in markets — large and small — all across the nation, a condition that did not significantly change for 50 more years.

Several weeks went by before Alan returned to the Chamber of Commerce. He then announced that the D-day of June 1, 1952, was coming closer, and the great "Freeze" of 1948 (something I'd never heard about before, but which had enormous impact on the development of free-to-the-viewer, over-the-air television) was about to thaw. We should start getting ready to make an application. Now it was beginning to get real, and I asked the question I should have asked earlier, "How much is all this going to take, Al?"

"Maybe half a million dollars. Gotta buy a lot of stuff, fill out a

Al Tindal makes a pitch for local recognition at the Springfield Advertising Club in 1953.

bunch of forms. We should get going, soon. There's gonna be two channels in the Springfield/Holyoke area."

I gulped — Aunt Elsie hadn't left all that much for me, less than five percent of what Al was mentioning. So, that night I called my father, figuring that's what fathers are for — providing help when wayward sons need it. He was in Washington at the time, working for a dollar-a-year as President Truman's Economic Stabilizer during the Korean "Police Action." I knew he had a long-standing distaste for the local newspaper monopoly, because he felt their then-owner, Sherman Hoar Bowles (1888–1952), had treated him unfairly during the five pre-war years when he had been mayor of Springfield. I explained the situation I had gotten myself into, asking for his wisdom and help: "I've either got to tell Al Tindal the truth real quick, or you'll have to help rescue me."

(Our original black and white studio cameras weighed almost one hundred pounds and cost around $20,000 apiece in 1952. Nowadays our

WWLP personality display in the Main Street window of Third National Bank — Bill Rasmussen, John Quill, Ed Kennedy, Bill Putnam, Harry Robator, and Keith Silver.

grandchildren have the electronic equivalent — but in living color — and swing it from a wrist strap, at a cost of less than one percent, despite the intervening inflation of currency. Those GE cameras we bought [and the comparable Dumonts we soon came to acquire] were massive affairs, each requiring a cable about an inch in diameter which connected the studio heads to a full rack of backup electronics apiece; they used numerous hot tubes and were perpetually in need of adjustment and fine-tuning. For every person actually manning a camera head, another was required in the control room to make sure the beast kept steady. Transmitters used a comparable complement of hot tubes, but soon became a great deal more stable, so that the FCC later came to retract its rule about having a first-class engineer on perpetual transmitter duty.)

"Gregor," the self-inflicted internal family name for Roger Lowell Putnam (1893–1972), was fully up to this challenge I had come into; it

Iconoscope cameras in 1954, for films and slides (rack of commercials at extreme left).

turned out to be something he really approved of, and he clearly felt this would be a sufficient long-term opportunity for his second son, the most adventurous of his six children. He would make a few phone calls and fly home for the following weekend.

Sitting around in his living room on Saturday, a group of his business associates rapidly coalesced around the theme of Springfield Television Broadcasting Corporation (later to be abbreviated by excising the word "Broadcasting"), in which WSPR, Tindal's radio station, would be a minority shareholder, contributing no money, but whatever of his station personnel we could use and his contacts in the broadcasting industry. The largest investor and initial president would be my father; his longtime personal lawyer, Ray King, would be the clerk and get us incorporated; Al would be vice-president; I would be the treasurer. Several of my father's and my business associates would ante up and become our initial board of directors. Over the years, our board came to be more reflective of the other persons who put in capital, as well as a significant representation of the other communities where we came to operate stations — Dayton and Salt Lake City.

Since it turned out that nobody else knew more about how to apply for a television station construction permit than I did, I was also named interim CEO. Gregor would return to Washington on Sunday evening and nail down suitable counsel to handle the actual filing with the FCC. Kitty and I returned to work at the chamber, where the general manager, Tom Fitzgerald, an old political friend of the family, promptly asked if he could buy a few shares. Thereafter, he looked upon our occasional absences with a blind eye — a local TV station would surely be a good chamber member to be friendly with.

Thus it was that for the next several weeks, Kitty had plenty of typing homework in compiling data and then neatly filling out the FCC forms

The other founding investors in Springfield Television, clockwise from Roger Putnam; George Vadnais, Dr. Charles L. Furcolo, James Y. Scott, Alan C. Tindal, John Oakley, Joseph J. Deliso, Raymond T. King.

to show that we were all reputable citizens, and that we were blessed with sufficient resources to build and operate a station. Meanwhile, I got to spend evenings drawing profiles based on Geological Survey topographic maps, and weekends traipsing through the late-winter snow on whatever high spots we might hope to obtain for our transmitter location. In the end, this turned out to be land actually owned by the City of Springfield's Water Department (Provin Mountain) west across the Connecticut River in the township of Agawam, the nearest high point to Springfield on a discontinuous basaltic ridge that ran the 100-mile length of the lower Connecticut River valley and on an element of which every FM and TV broadcaster from New Haven northward already had his antenna, or wished he had.

Over subsequent years, our frequent internal as well as on-the-air references to "the mountain" gave this 640-foot elevation a much greater stature than it deserved. Our landlord, the Springfield Water Department, maintained a set of enormous tanks, sufficient to supply the "head" and two days' worth of water to the city and some of its suburbs, somewhat lower and about a mile to the north of WWLP. (The tale of Springfield's unique, super-soft, gravity-fed, electricity-generating water supply system is a deserving saga in its own right. The City had acquired most of the mile-long ridge more than a century earlier, incidental to the process of building this system, but we paid more in annual rent for our 4.5 acres than the City had paid to purchase the whole mile-and-a-half-long mountain.)

That portion of the long, trap-rock ridge had another claim to fame. Along its full length in the township of Agawam there was a foot path, somewhat maintained by the Appalachian Mountain Club and named the Metacomet Trail, which ran from Mount Monadnock in New Hampshire south to the cliffs near New Haven in Connecticut. I was a life member of that club, the oldest and largest mountaineering organization west of the Atlantic Ocean, and soon to be one of its officers. But it was Metacomet that interested me, and we came to care for the segment of trail that crossed our land on Provin Mountain. Metacomet, known to the whites as King Philip, was the son and successor of Massasoit, the Wampanoag chief who had welcomed the *Mayflower* Pilgrims in 1620, and was invited to the first Thanksgiving "feast" a year later. It was also Metacomet who belatedly found that the native's concept of shared land use (actual ownership resting forever with the Great Spirit) was fundamentally alien to the immigrant's culture — the Pilgrims misinterpreted the Wampanoag chief's willingness to share the land as a series of exclusive transfers. When many more shiploads of English arrived and much of the better food-growing terrain of southern New England had thus become fenced (or stonewalled) off into farms, with all access being denied to the prior inhabitants, King Philip launched a year-long military effort to regain access to what his people had lost. Ultimately Metacomet came off second best in that costly war, which ended in 1676, though meanwhile his braves had burned Springfield and killed many settlers. Finally, he was traitorously captured, then hanged, drawn and quartered — in the time-honored English fashion — with his head exhibited in Plymouth, and his wife and baby son were sold into slavery in the West Indies. His is a sad and complicated story, but it carries a strong message about fair play and conservation.

Being a bit of a conservationist, as well as somewhat stingy, I put such lugubrious thoughts of Metacomet aside, for there was nothing I could do to repair that damage, and soon planned to save on capital and operating costs by co-locating our studio with the transmitter. All transmitters are inefficient and generate much heat, along with whatever they are supposed to transmit. In those early days, a television transmitter turned up to 75 percent of its electric energy input into heat. We used this surplus heat to warm the building, thus saving on a furnace, and we also, therefore, did not have to install any permanent microwave link from elsewhere. The FCC, it turned out, liked to have its licensees maintain their principal studios within the "City of License," but — on any reasonable showing — would readily grant waivers of this rule. As time went on, we more than made up for this exception, through extensive use of our soon-to-be-purchased mobile studio unit.

The Commission's main concern in adopting its *Sixth Report and Table of Television Allocations*, was to ensure the technical availability of at least one broadcast channel to every sizeable community across the nation. Of course, the Commission's staff, being on the public payroll (but none of them ever having had to meet one), worked out everything in theory, but precious little bureaucratic thought had been given to any realistic thinking about what future equipment developments or private initiative might do with the economic aspects of the vast radiated power limitations that were also included (up to 100 Kw for "low band" VHF stations, and 316 Kw for stations in the "high band," on channels 7 through 13). Nor had there been much thought about the delayed impact of its unnecessarily long four-year "freeze." Even the relatively minor and occasionally snowbound City of Flagstaff came out of the staff's plan with four television channel allocations, two of which were in the UHF band.

In order to achieve "parity" of coverage with the lower channel stations, UHF stations were originally allowed to radiate a maximum of 1,000,000 Kw, later raised to 5,000,000 Kw; but then, of course, they had to pay a correspondingly higher electric power bill. When UHF stations first went on the air, the highest radiated power then attainable was somewhat less than 250,000 watts, which was achieved by use of a 12-kilowatt transmitter and an antenna gain of 25 — discounted by some 15 percent, for transmission line loss. But the equipment manufacturers were quick to design and peddle transmission systems for the Vs that reached their allotted maxima.

In the longer run, moving past the great economic leg up given the 108 pre-freeze stations, the question of "market preservation" came to dominate the internal discussions and regulation of the television broadcasting industry — a condition that was greatly complicated by the growth of CATV — cable television — a "service" that unanimously — at first anyway — imported the signals from distant, larger-market stations, often duplicating much of the programming of local stations. Thus, smaller-market stations, with a smaller revenue base to start with, were even further disadvantaged, for the process of importation was never the other way around. Smaller-market stations, with their lower economic base, were even further disadvantaged by the frequent loss of good talent to stations in larger markets, which could afford to pay correspondingly higher salaries. Communities such as the market area of Flagstaff could have supported one or more local stations, but for the public's never-ending desire for greater variety of television, which only a couple of stations could never hope to supply.

As Tindal had stated, according to the FCC's *Sixth Report* on television allocations, there were two channels to be available in Springfield, 55 and 61. So, rather than risk the potential delay of a comparative hearing, we opted for the higher frequency, for we already knew — I was learning the internal gossip of the broadcasting business fast — that a local media group, somewhat oriented toward Holyoke, was preparing an application for Channel 55. What none of us appreciated was that in this evolving medium, not one home receiver in the entire nation could tune to either channel (save for a very few in the vicinity of Bridgeport, where an experimental station on a UHF channel had briefly operated) but they could all receive the signals — albeit often snowy — from any pre-freeze TV broadcasters, like the station in New Haven, WNHC-TV, which had been on the air for most of the previous four years, and was due to change from Channel 6 to Channel 8 in the course of implementing the new allocations plan. It was this ignorant optimism which got us into television, but naively — we had no hint of the long, lean period of shoveling against the tide, hard work, worry and woe that lay ahead of us.

As the new allocations plan was implemented, we were terribly distressed when the chairman of Agawam's Board of Selectmen (to whose political entity we paid our property taxes) took it upon himself to write to the FCC urging the Commission to delay enforcing this channel switch, for we knew that the great frequency difference between Channels 6 and 8 would require new home receiving antennae and thus bring about a substantial increase in our potential viewership, a point we had hoped was clear to a businessman like Fred Emerson. Naturally (and fortunately) the FCC ignored him, for there were other channel switches that were tied into that required for WNHC-TV.

I was soon to learn the rules for frequency assignments and much of the table of UHF (and VHF) allocations, backwards and forwards. Co-channel separations in the more densely populated Northeast were based on a minimum spacing between transmitters of 160 airline miles; adjacent channels were to be separated by 60 miles and there were other lesser but arcane separations required due to receiver interference oscillations. In due course our chief engineer and I were able to dope out a series of minor re-allocations that enabled us to switch down from Channel 61 to 22, thereby more than doubling our potential audience overnight — but that's another story — also to come.

Most of the enormous-sounding wattage that television broadcasters radiate is derived from what is called "antenna gain," a means whereby the radiated signal is flattened out from the circular "figure 8" of a dipole, to attain more of a pancake pattern so as to reach where people actually live, not waste a lot of energy down into the mountaintop or out into space. The "gain" is a term of art expressed in the degree of flattening from "1" in the original and theoretical "8" — to something between 20 and 50 times.

We were not the only UHF optimists in Massachusetts. There was another bunch who occupied the top of Asnebumskit Hill in Paxton, a northwesterly suburb of Worcester, Springfield's rival for the second city title in Massachusetts. Unfortunately, the shareholders of Salisbury Broadcasting, licensees of WWOR, on Channel 14, had to compete with the several VHF signals (Channels 4, 7, 10 and 12) coming from Boston and Providence, a condition which forced them to go dark at about the same time that WWLP was edging firmly into the black. The networks were unanimously willing — when necessary — to place their programs in marginal time slots on those existing VHF stations, rather than allow them live clearance on WWOR. Anything not so placed — which was precious little — was available. We encountered an updated variation of this same condition in the City of Dayton, a dozen years later, but by then, the All-Channel Receiver Law was in effect.

Other than their equipment, some of it still mortgaged to RCA and their license, these people had another asset, an operating loss-carry-forward of some $700,000. So, we dickered with them and RCA for a while and finally arranged for the Salisbury stockholders to merge into and ultimately acquire 10 percent of Springfield Television. Two of Salisbury's principals came onto our board of directors, John Z. Buckley and Kenneth P. Higgins, and we took over another mountaintop, soon changing the call letters to WJZB.

Asnebumskit Hill is a very prominent part of the central Massachusetts landscape, north of the Worcester airport, and it already had a noteworthy place in the history of broadcasting, for it was one of the two transmitter locations for the Yankee Network's early and unfortunately unsuccessful foray into FM broadcasting. The other location was in northern New Hampshire, on the top of Mount Washington, home of the "Worst Weather on Earth" and a spot which I had visited quite often during some of my misspent youth. By utilizing these two very prominent elevated sites, Yankee had been able to beam a clear FM signal into almost all parts of New England, and much of the adjacent province of Quebec. Its abandoned, Eiffel-style tower, identical to and as sturdy as its structure on the famously windswept top of Mount Washington, stood only a few dozen yards south of the equally sturdy masonry building that our Worcester friends had remodeled to serve as the studios and offices of WWOR. This was in much the same manner that we had put our all into structures on the top of Provin Mountain in Agawam, except that Asnebumskit Hill was more than twice as high above sea-level, and from its crest, on a good day, one could actually see the taller buildings in Boston.

Other than its news programs, which it declared a "public service," NBC would not go with us to this other station; its affiliate in Boston was sufficiently persuasive that we could not program WJZB as we did our nearly simultaneous satellite station in southwestern New Hampshire, WRLP. Thus, the FCC staff's dream of having every major city in the country able to support several TV outlets, which lay behind the adoption of the UHF TV band, was defeated, and Worcester became, in effect, a TV suburb of Boston, though its local newspaper, the Worcester *Telegram & Gazette*, was quite profitable and operated very popular local radio stations, WTAG AM and FM (until it was all acquired by the *New York Times* in more recent years).

Since it cost us very little to keep the station on the air with minimal hours of operation, we further remodeled the venerable building and made it habitable for the family of one of our senior engineers, Jim McMahon, so they could live there for the several years we operated that station, which we did mostly at the subliminal urging of FCC Commissioner Lee, who did not want to have the electronic space occupied by Channel 14 (470 to 476 MHz) go completely unused, for fear it would become fair game for other potential users of the radio spectrum, and thus be another obstacle to maintenance of the UHF band for broadcasting. When the FCC finally found itself forced to allow for some sharing with other users of the lower UHF channels, we opted to save the money, and the station went dark again.

2

Actually Building a Station

[WLP] The Federal Communications Commission granted our application for a construction permit on July 1, 1952, its first official release after the end of the "freeze," and we moved fast, ordering everything from studio cameras (for Kitty) to beacon lights (for me) from the General Electric Company. Nobody had a UHF transmitter on the shelf somewhere for sale, but GE was promising one with a power output of twelve kilowatts, as opposed to the one-kilowatt job that RCA (the only other major equipment supplier) was offering, and on which Al had a purchasing priority. We did know one other thing — more of that quick study — the higher the frequency being used, the less desirable it was, for over-the-air propagation diminishes with higher frequencies. But we did not know that this difference also meant more serious issues with the 6AF4 tubes originally required in those heretofore nonexistent home receivers — that was to be another shocker. We were also to learn that pine and other "needle" trees were electronically toxic, for the water vapor and moisture held in their foliage was more intense and there all year long, while deciduous trees only cramped our signal in the summers.

But GE had yet other surprises in store for us. Having placed our (to us, anyway) enormous equipment order in early July, by late summer we were asking about delivery dates and were told, "Soon!" Come the autumn of 1952, RCA was already announcing delivery dates for their UHF transmitters, and we were getting increasingly anxious. Somehow, being first on the air had a sort of cachet that one could boast about, though we soon learned that people at home cared little about such things — a clear signal, ease of tuning and popular programs were far more conducive to viewer interest than air dates, diversity of ownership, the morals of the management, overlapping and/or diverse media ownerships and other intangibles that the FCC regularly said it cared about, but never

21

WWLP as it was first built in 1953 — the new film editing room projected out ten feet, between the downspouts on the right.

seemed to be very serious about enforcing. One of the earlier surprises we had coming to us was that the "exciter" part of GE's transmitter used several 4X150 tubes, which had the habit of burning out with some regularity and had to be checked (often replaced) before sign-on each day. We made the front page of the local paper (which had managed to ignore our on-the-air date of March 17) when we ran through (and then out of) a batch of defective 4X150s and had to yell for help from GE. It responded by sending a crate of tubes by a special messenger from some New York area warehouse to New Haven by car, which I drove south to meet, before returning to the mountain — in less time than the speed laws permit on the much later Interstate Highway 91.

Anyhow, after the GE salesman promised us a March 1st delivery date for the transmitter, and actually got most equipment in our hands well before that time, the employees of Lemuel Boulware (GE's then vice-president for labor relations) called his bluff and went out on strike, just when we were ready to install our diplexer and a second final power-amplifying "klystron" tube. Everything we absolutely had to have was

Top: Our first non-test transmission — March 10, 1953, received at the home of Lewis Richmond —18 miles from "the mountain." *Bottom:* Springfield Television's stations dual logo in 1957. WWLP (and its companion stations — WRLP and WJZB) used several versions of the same basic station logo.

Chief Engineer George Townsend (second from left) explains the innards of a klystron amplifier to FCC engineering bureaucrats.

stuck in the factory "for the duration." In the meantime, studio and film cameras (using such strange names as "image orthicon" and "iconoscope") were being assembled by our engineers and back-up electronics were being installed into racks in the WSPR studio building, before being loaded — again into the backs of big station wagons (salesman Phil Rennison's Buick and my Chrysler) for transport up to the mountain, where our studio and some minimal office space were also being built. This was sometimes a hazardous venture, traveling on an unpaved, poorly-graded, often muddy mountain road, but gradually we got it all up there and to work.

Among the personnel that came with the WSPR connection was its chief engineer, the late George Rhodes Townsend, an enormously talented man whose tireless ingenuity bailed us out of many a tight spot. Most broadcasters hired a Washington-based consulting engineer to run the final "proof of performance" for their official "license"—as opposed to a "temporary operating permit." But Townsend, a World War II Navy communications Chief Petty Officer, was able to do it all himself and WWLP was the first UHF station to receive a permanent license.

Upon receipt of the dire news about a strike from GE, George allowed that maybe, for a while, we could get by without a diplexer (an electronic

Our beloved treasurer, Roland L. Filiault, who always managed to keep us afloat.

WWLP management is saluted at the Chamber of Commerce Breakfast Club on St. Patrick's Day, 1953.

mixing device that blends the audio with the video so that both elements of a television signal can travel in the same waveguide or coaxial line) to the antenna. There are other means of accomplishing this same end and George figured that he could rig a separate antenna for the audio, which we could side-mount on our shiny new tower. So, on March 10, 1953, I arranged with the GE salesman for the loan of a small segment of helical antenna, and then drove west on US Route 20 through the night in my hefty station wagon to Syracuse, where all that gear was made. The two items we needed were already on the shipping dock, so a couple of beefy managerial personnel helped load the more delicate klystron into the back of my car and lash the carefully padded eight-foot segment of helical antenna onto the roof. And I was off for "the mountain," and our date with history, one week later, on St. Patrick's Day.

That tower was the start of a long relationship with Henry Guzewicz and his engineering older brother, Walter, Stainless Tower makers of Binghamton, and with a tower rigger, Raymond Mercier, of near Croton, New York. We came by them both through conversations with the GE salesman, and never turned back. They gave us perpetual satisfaction. But there was an early moment of uncertainty with Mercier.

Our first Guzewicz tower arrived as sixteen 20-foot segments stacked onto a couple of flatbed trucks, which had to struggle up the questionable road past the Water Department and almost a mile south along the ridge to its top. Once we had its concrete footings in place, the tower arrived on the mountain simultaneously with Mercier, his winch truck, and his assistant, who promptly got to work. Several days later, Ray had everything in place and called down to the office to ask the company's real treasurer, Roland Filiault, to cut his check. But Roland told him he would get nothing until I had approved the job. So Ray went looking for me, and finally glanced up at his freshly finished tower, down which I was slowly climbing, having checked every bolt and hanger. When I set foot on the ground, several minutes later, Ray gave me a scathing look and asked how I liked his work.

"It all looks OK to me," I responded.

"Well! Now will you authorize my payment?" The rigger was clearly upset.

"Right away," I replied.

More than a dozen years and several tower jobs later, Ray Mercier and I were enjoying a beer after he had finished his final tower project for us.

"You know, Bill, you're the only station owner I've ever met who personally inspected a tower job on me. I'm fully insured, you know."

"Ray, the phone doesn't ring when I'm several hundred feet up in the air; Kitty handles everything just fine while I'm enjoying the fresh air and a bit of exercise. And though I know and trust you, I'm not afraid of heights and I like to be certain I know what's going on in all parts of this business — particularly to make sure that the beacon assembly is bolted on firmly 'cause I get to change its bulbs, and — did you know that I also bail out the septic tank?"

Over time, with numerous passing thunderstorms and associated lightning strikes, such exalted beacons tend to become covered with zap marks (like warts), and often the 500-watt lightbulbs, of which there are two, explode, creating a bit of a mess inside the beacon. I can attest that there are more pleasant tasks than swinging in the breeze atop the more more than 50-foot "Lally column" of an antenna — some hundreds of feet above ground in the predawn winter cold — to lift open the hinged top half of the beacon and then clean out glass shards before one can change a couple of defunct lightbulbs.

That final tower job came about tragically. A private plane pilot had left Buffalo, New York, for Keene, New Hampshire, and neglected to correct his altimeter when approaching for a landing. His mistake was deadly, for when he arrived in the clouds over Gun Hill, south of Keene, he was more than a thousand feet below where he should have been and clipped the tower at WRLP, our then satellite station in southwestern New Hampshire. After breaking one of the south guy wires, the plane impacted the tower itself and left it with a pronounced kink near the 400-foot level, knocking our station off the air and terminating the pilot's life.

Upon learning of this event, I promptly called Ray to come inspect and advise on the situation. He showed up the very next day and, after a studious look with binoculars at the obviously severely wounded tower, Ray said there was only one solution — dump the tower and start over again; no rigger would dare undertake an attempt at repair. Ray's solution for the ensuing dump was simple. He gathered the remaining four guy wires that were attached to the south anchor into one large shackle. He then applied his cutting torch to the shackle until it broke, whereupon the tower curled over, reminding me of a chambered nautilus, the tortured metal screeching loudly as the antenna fell, beacon first, into the forest. It left a bit of a mess in the woods which took us some time to clean up; but we got good money from the local scrap dealer for the sadly mangled copper coax, though very little for the crumpled steel.

In its several years on the air, that station had never turned a profit, no matter how we adjusted the accounting, so I debated rebuilding, figuring that the substantial insurance settlement would be sufficient heart balm. Roland had already determined that the pilot's liability policy and our own station property insurance carriers were one and the same, so there could be no finger pointing in approving our claim. We opted to make our claim under the late pilot's policy because it had the larger limits. I would have taken the tragic disaster as a favorable economic sign from above, but FCC Commissioner Bob Lee, our patron, whom I immediately consulted on the matter, insisted we rebuild the station as rapidly as possible. WRLP, on Channel 32, occupied another frequency 578–584 MHz of which he didn't want other FCC spectrum users to become unduly covetous.

With a new tower at WRLP soon in place, we had to face the painting issue, which meant a predawn climb to the antenna. Thus, early one Saturday morning in June, armed with a huge number of my climbing slings and carabiners and accompanied by my teenaged son, Lowell, who had been attuned to climbing almost from birth, and a friend of his for company and assistance, we drove north and climbed up the tower, stationing extra buckets of paint at convenient spots. Then, I went farther up the new 60-foot antenna to the beacon, some 590 feet in the air, at the crack of dawn on a very pleasant morning, before the station had signed back on the air, and started painting my way down the antenna. My paint

John Fergie poses beside the concrete base for the 600-foot WRLP towers on Gun Hill in Winchester, NH.

bucket contained only international orange, for the antenna, while the boys below me were using white on the topmost segment of the new tower.

When I had painted down to join them, we each took one face of the tower, so as to avoid — as much as possible — painting each other, for the rest of the way down. With a gentle breeze blowing from the northwest, most of the stray drops of paint served to decorate the newly opened leaves on the oak trees far below, but it was several days and many showers later before we were all cleansed from that long day's work. In the course of this endeavor, Lowell's friend, Gene Boss (aka "Craw" from some childhood inanity), later to be our personal physician, managed to drag out the telling of one joke for more than one hundred feet as we painted our way down to the ground.

At least one of the early problems we had to live with was totally out of our control. In those primitive days of television, the network interconnections, with audio and video traveling separately, came through AT&T, and occasionally the service provided by Ma Bell (or "the Octopus," depending on your prejudices) was subject to failure. They, too, used hot tubes and equipment that didn't always perform as advertised. But we had enough troubles of our own, for which we received regular lambastings from our viewers, sponsors and competitors, and didn't feel the need to take any heat when the AT&T microwave link from the network to WWLP went down. So, we devised a balop slide that read simply "*Telephone Company Service Failure*" and put it on the air whenever the AT&T connection failed. It wasn't a fancy piece of artwork, but it was to the point, and we put it up when appropriate.

Then, one day in the late summer of 1953, some big shots from Ma Bell's regional headquarters in Boston, headed by a dignified vice-president, the late Fearing Pratt, came to call. They didn't like our slide.

"What's wrong with it?" we asked, knowing it was not complimentary, but begging the question of what we knew their real mission to be.

"We think it's misleading, and our Legal Department says you can be stopped from using that message."

"You guys want us to put a bell [their logo] on it?" Townsend asked, with a straight face. They were not amused.

I suggested that if they looked far enough back into the corporate records they would find my name (my grandfather [1862–1924], for whom I was named, was the first general counsel for the American Telephone and Telegraph Company — when it was based in Boston) and that I was not going to be buffaloed into taking a hit for their shortcomings.

In the end, Mr. Pratt and his associates got the message; whenever their service failed, they would get free "advertising" from us. Very soon, however, their microwave link from John Tom Hill in Connecticut to "the mountain" received a back-up transmitter and we were able to retire the offending slide.

One of our earlier allies in the UHF wars for survival was the late Thomas P. Chisman, CEO of WVEC-TV, initially licensed to operate on Channel 15 in Norfolk, Virginia. One day, when Kitty was down in the studio, I got a call from someone and needed to refer to some correspondence we'd had with Tom. So I looked in the correspondence file under Chisman — nothing; under WVEC — again nothing; under UHF — more nothing; and I finally gave up, pending Kitty's return from the studio.

The moment she came through the office door, I started to upbraid her for having such a slipshod filing system, until she went to the file cabinet and promptly pulled out a folder labeled "Peninsula."

"Here!" She handed me the folder. "The name of Tom's company is 'Peninsula Broadcasting.'"

And so it was, in small print at the bottom of the letterhead in the latest communication from Tom. But thereafter, whenever I couldn't find something she had put away, I had a standard line about it probably being filed under "Peninsula."

A Later, Midwinter, Construction Project

Translators were a concept that originated in Colorado, to fill in the Denver stations' coverage area down in the western valleys of that mountainous state. The FCC was very reluctant to give legal status to these devices, but came under enormous political pressure from Colorado's governor,

Edwin Carl Johnson, a former three-term United States senator (who forced the issue when he began to give out appropriate licenses from the state), and it finally, in the late 1950s, made them legal. This new status applied only to the uppermost UHF channels, though a good many of these devices, particularly in the West, continued to operate on other frequencies. Since WWLP held an increasingly valuable license, we were reluctant to flout FCC authority and so waited until these low-power devices were legal before entertaining the idea of actually building and owning them.

We ended up with two translators to enhance the coverage area of WRLP, the satellite station on Channel 32 that we came to build in southwestern New Hampshire; the second of which devices — on Channel 81— was a two-day, midwinter saga, early in 1958. George Townsend, Ralph Jay, our most versatile staff engineer, and I assembled everything we would need — some of it, particularly the more delicate electronic stuff, in the back of my station wagon, but the great bulk of the material and tools we needed (including some dry cordwood) was packed into the station's 4x4 heavy-duty Dodge pickup truck, complete with front-end winch. Bob Vadnais (about whom, more below) had pre-fabricated an eight-by-eight-foot cubic shack (using a dozen sheets of plywood and numerous 2x3 joists) for the electronic gear to fit into, and we had purchased a one-foot-on-each-side tower of 60 feet total height — in six ten-foot segments.

On the appointed February day, the three of us set out early for the north country, aiming to arrive by noon on the assigned hilltop, near an airways beacon, across the Connecticut River from the Lebanon Airport, on the high ground south of the White River. The snow was nearly three feet deep in the town of Hartford (Vermont) when we left my car down near the highway (not far from the junction of what would later be I-91 and I-93) and started plowing our way up that hill in the sturdy Dodge truck. We bucked and plowed along various abandoned country roads until the snow became too deep for even our well-equipped vehicle. At this juncture, in the late morning, we unfastened the plow blade and managed to go another few hundred yards, with just the truck's own four-wheel-drive agility — until we came to the final upgrade. Here, despite use of the low-range gearbox and chains all around, we lost all traction and were stymied, until Ralph suggested we try using the winch. So he and George dragged the end of the cable up the hillside and fastened its chain about the base of a big pine tree near the crest (and that airways

Kitty stands beside some second-generation videotape machines.

An early videotape machine; Bob Vadnais also made the cabinets for storing tapes, at left.

beacon). I started to take up the slack with the winch and the heavily laden truck slowly began to inch its way up the hillside once more.

Then, the ancient lane steepened, the truck just couldn't, and I began to fear we would break the winch's shear pin. But by now we had managed to get more than halfway up that final grade, so George suggested we try doubling the cable — passing it around the pine tree and back down to the front bumper of the truck. We rerigged the cable accordingly and started, even more slowly, up the hill again, as the cable began to saw its way into the tree. Just before noon, we got to the unforested crest of the hilltop, near the beacon, and were able to unload the truck.

I left George and Ralph to dig out the snow down to the ground and set about bolting together Bob's diminutive pre-fab house, while I used the pathway we had so laboriously created to take the truck down to the highway again for the other material we had left locked in my car. An hour later, I was back, this time traveling on a well-beaten path, to find the pre-fab house mostly assembled and fires burning on the sites George and Ralph had selected to place the guy anchors for the tower.

By sunset, we had dug the anchor holes in the largely unfrozen soil and poured a concrete mix to hold the tower's guy wires, which we were all set to erect the next morning. The engineers had also managed to "borrow" a bit of electricity from the line that supplied the beacon. Fortunately, the temperature did not fall too low that night, as the three of us snuggled into sleeping bags on the floor, after eating a dinner which Kitty had sent along to ensure our survival. However, among the items Bob Vadnais had built into our "house" was a sturdy clip, such as might hold a small fire extinguisher, but which our borrowed light disclosed was actually holding a greenish bottle. Finally, after a spell of fruitless inquiries of my bunkmates, curiosity overcame discomfort and I reached up out of my sleeping bag to see what this unexplained container actually was.

Bob, a native of Quebec, in his thoughtfulness, had sent along a bottle of imported Geneva gin to ease the hard and uninsulated plywood floor of our sleeping arrangements!

3

Lowering Our Frequency — Overnight

[WLP] The earliest UHF home tuners made (back in 1952–1955) used a triode tube — many examples of which proved to be unreliable and/or completely unresponsive at the higher frequencies, while generally working happily on the lower channels. In due course the 6AF4 came to be replaced with solid state resistors, but that was a lot later, and their unreliability soon became widely recognized as detrimental to viable UHF station operation, particularly on the higher frequencies. Channel 61 was one of those frequencies, and since WWLP used the highest such channel (752–758 MH) anywhere in the country, we felt the issue most severely. George Townsend and I began to study the FCC's Table of Allocations, with a view to improving our channel number by lowering it and thus gaining audience.

We had observed that a number of home receivers in Springfield could bring in the picture from WKNB-TV on Channel 30, licensed to New Britain, Connecticut (a station with its antenna five times farther away than ours, and operating with a one-kilowatt transmitter), better than they could get our signal from a much nearer transmission point and with more than ten times the radiated power. This would never do! The FCC's published Table of Television Allocations assigned co-channels in the UHF-TV band with quite a bit of slack, beyond the mandatory 160 airline miles. There was an operating station (a CBS affiliate) on Channel 22 in Scranton, Pennsylvania, and unused allocations for the same frequency in Bar Harbor, Maine, as well as one that was later implemented in Burlington, Vermont. Yet there was sufficient slack that one could also be assigned in southern New England. So we proposed a reallocation of unused frequency assignments affecting various communities, mostly in southern New England, a reallocation which even allowed our local competitor, WHYN-TV, an ABC affiliate (then owned by a collage of the local daily print media: 50 percent by the Springfield Newspapers soon to be acquired by Newhouse); 30 percent by the (soon to be late) Holyoke *Transcript* and Greenfield *Recorder*, and 20 percent by the owners of the venerable Northampton *Gazette,*) to switch down fifteen channels, if it wished, which it eventually did. Indeed, some years later, when most of the issues surrounding UHF-TV operation had been solved, albeit often quite painfully, and we had left broadcasting, Channel 61 became much more viable and was taken up in Hartford as an affiliate of the Fox Network.

The FCC granted our rule-making and soon gave us the necessary "show cause" order to shift from Channel 61 down to 22 at 518–524 MH. On the appointed early July day in the summer of 1955, with a new antenna and lots of replacement coaxial line already on hand, Ray Mercier showed up to complete the switch at the top of our soon-to-be-some-what-overloaded original tower. We took this opportunity to replace the three-inch copper coaxial line with the larger and more expensive six-inch variety, which was also much more efficient and improved the strength of the signal actually reaching the antenna. When Ray had completed the antenna switch and removed his gin pole (all in the dark after midnight), he and his assistant started on the "coax," replacing each 20-foot segment of the old line, but in view of our time limitations on that dark and foggy night, only affixing three (of the six) bolts at each junction. George Townsend, who did not mind heights (having often swung from the masts of a wave-tossed destroyer during the late war), was busy inside the building with more sophisticated technical matters, the diplexer and klystron tube changes, so I took over completion of the coax job and began working my way down from the top of the tower, putting in the other three coax bolts, tightening each coupling joint securely, and checking all the spring-loaded hangers.

Our then assistant chief engineer, Don Shaw, had a well-advertised fear of heights and had pointedly never set foot on the tower — even on the bottom rung. When I arrived down near the 220-foot level, I heard Don's familiar voice somewhat below me; he was also putting in missing bolts, but talking to someone on the ground.

"Don," I asked, "do you know where you are?"

"Nope," he replied, "in all this fog and darkness I'm just as happy if I don't know, so please don't tell me."

The whole job was completed without a hitch, though largely in almost total darkness, and when WWLP signed on for the *Today Show* at 0700 on the morning of July 2, 1955, our potential audience had more than doubled.

The only complication in it all had occurred to my older brother, Roger, Jr, who was drafted for the occasion to help revise some of the plumbing pertinent to the new (and larger) water-cooled klystron tubes necessary for the lower frequency. He was lying on his side under the radiator unit of one heat exchanger, sweating copper pipe connections, when one of the two goats I had obtained, hopefully to do lawn work around the station, poked his head inside the air intake opening and, fancying the seat of my brother's pants edible, took a good nip at his butt.

These goats were one of my less successful ideas for operating economy. It turned out that they didn't care for grass at all, preferring the shrubbery, even oak trees (they would pair up — one to hold a small tree down and the other to munch off its leaves) to what I had hoped would be their diet. They also wandered the entire premises, butting in doors as needed, so as to make free with Kitty's living room set overnight (much to her highly vocal distress), and leaving their "calling cards" everywhere. About this same time, Kitty's growls about these animals turned into a more distinct roar when the insurgent goats tipped over a bottle of ammonia during one of her live interviews.

After we tended to my brother's wounded dignity, the critters' departure for a different domicile was widely applauded.

◆   ◆   ◆

A Downwind Lander

As soon as Roland felt we were financially able, we set out to replace our original stainless tower, which we felt sure was now unsafely overloaded, and took counsel with Walter Guzewicz on the matter. The new tower, being a great deal heftier, arrived in many more pieces than the original, but assembling the whole thing was no issue for Mercier, and within a week, we were radiating a few more kilowatts from a few feet higher; but we also had a pile of used tower for sale, exactly 280 feet of it stacked on the ground.

So we placed a small ad in *Broadcasting*, and soon found a buyer, who

WWLP really took to the air in 1960, courtesy of shareholder Morrill Stone Ring and his Beech Bonanza.

flew up from Georgia in his private plane and then paid us the pittance we asked. However, he was unwise enough to land (flying with the wind) at the Bowles-Agawam Airport near the mountain. Unfortunately, the man's plane stayed for several weeks, near the end of that strip, its undercarriage sadly tangled in a fence line, though the plane was basically uninjured. The owner managed to arrange a repair deal with the resident mechanics at Bowles-Agawam and then took a commercial flight from Bradley Field back to Atlanta; but that was not the end of the story.

A number of weeks later, George Townsend, Kitty and I flew to Chicago in the Beech Bonanza owned by one of our larger shareholders, Morrill Stone Ring, a local nursing home owner/operator, to attend the annual meeting of the National Association of Broadcasters. While circling for a landing at Miegs Field, near the lake, I noticed there was a plane at the end of the runway that seemed to be canted sideways and immobile. When I pointed it out to him, Morrill then asked the tower controller what the story about that aircraft was.

Back crackled the voice from the tower: "It belongs to some character from Georgia, who's up here for the Broadcaster's convention, but hasn't even got a station on the air. He made a downwind landing here last night...."

4

Parentheses

[WLP] The late Frank Back, a 1938 immigrant from Austria, produced the first Zoom lenses for television. The chief salesman for Back's Zoomar Corporation was a courtly gentleman named Jack Pegler, a relative of the right-wing news commentator (Francis James) Westbrook Pegler (1894–1969). Jack was accustomed to demonstrating the beauties of his lenses for television cameras, at every trade show and in between. In 1955, still optimistically betting on ultimate prosperity, WWLP acquired Universal Zoomar lens #007 from him and used it with pride at every opportunity.

Video tape machines were the invention of Charles Paulson Ginsberg (1920–1992) and first manufactured by the Ampex Corporation; they were (when they first came out — in 1954) expensive, bulky and clumsy. They used tape that was two inches wide and required four spinning heads to record data, as well as to retrieve it. When such a machine acquired even the smallest speck of dirt on one of those heads, it caused wide, snowy bands to appear across the resulting picture. At WWLP we built a special "clean" room for our first, $50,000, video tape machines. Without the capacity to record events for a later telecast, such as my editorials or Kitty's special guests, not to mention most of our locally originated commercials, we would not have had the flexibility that makes modern television possible.

Getting into color was another landmark step for any station. It was easy to transmit network originations. This required very little enhancement of our transmitter; but, though pressed by NBC, then a division of General Sarnoff's RCA, the foremost color receiver manufacturer, we decided to go slowly about originations. Films, slides and tape came next, so our local news had much color in it before we had studio cameras.

However, by 1962, all our local talent, led by Kitty, were clamoring for them, and advertiser pressures were building up; we finally had to do something. I approached an equipment maker from Indiana, Sarkes Tarzian (1900–1987), who also operated a UHF TV station, in Bloomington, Indiana, so I had to be his supporter, though he was far from the first manufacturer to offer color cameras.

"When are you going to produce a color studio camera, Sarkes?" I asked at one NAB Convention.

"As soon as we can, Bill; Biagio Presti is back home working on them, right now."

"Well, I'd like to get a couple for Springfield, and then two more for Dayton. There are all sorts of bad guys selling them here, but I'd rather do business with you, if it's at all possible. So please get cracking."

Several weeks later, I ran into Sarkes in the waiting room of Commissioner Lee's office in Washington and inquired again about the matter; increased pressure from our Sales Department was adding emphasis to Kitty's more polite queries.

"When are you gonna get me those cameras, Sarkes?"

"Presti is working night and day on them, Bill, probably before the next NAB."

"Keerist, Sarkes! I can't wait that long. I like Presti, but can't you just put a few more men on the job?"

"Bill! Some things just take time. No matter how many good men you put on the job, it still takes nine months to make a baby."

Among the tribulations of UHF television people was the total lack of sympathy for our economic plight that seemed to affect the suppliers of films for broadcasting. The regional salesman for National Telefilm Associates was particularly irksome in his corporate unwillingness to ease our situation by adjusting payment schedules — so I decided to get even when I was approached by a representative of the Department of Justice inquiring as to our experience with the legally questionable and coercive practice of "Block Booking." At this time, as well as later, movie films were "sold" for exhibition in packages, some items of which were good and some less so — but the exhibitor station had to "buy" (but not necessarily use) them all — good and bad alike. This practice had been forbidden many years earlier in regard to movie theaters, but was something most telecasters, with our much larger appetite for films, had come to accept. However, I was still smarting from the NTA rebuff and agreed to testify in any upcoming trial.

Thus, early in 1962, pursuant to a subsequent *subpoena*, I presented myself at the Federal District Court of Southern New York, in downtown Manhattan, and was duly sworn to tell the truth, etc., in Docket #8850 being heard before the Honorable Archie Owen Dawson (1878–1964). After my very brief direct testimony was concluded, the late, London-born attorney for the film industry, Louis Nizer, began his cross examination. He opened with a long, complicated question that seemed to take him about two minutes to ask, and then demanded that I give him a simple "Yes" or "No," answer.

I turned up to Judge Dawson and asked, "Would it be permissible, sir, for me to answer that question on the installment plan?"

Down came the jurist's gavel. Bang! "Mr. Nizer, this court will recess for ten minutes so that you can formulate questions that are possible for me to understand, and for this witness to answer."

All the attorneys promptly got up and marched out the back of the courtroom, leaving me alone with Judge Dawson.

"Son!" the elderly jurist turned down to me, "I see that you are from Springfield. Would you, by any chance, know where Petersham is?"

"Yes, sir; I know the town quite well. My parents have a summer home there, and I spent many pleasant days growing up in Petersham."

"Did you possibly know of Judge John Woolsey?"

"Why, yes, sir; he was our neighbor. My mother often sent me to pick blueberries in one of his overgrown fields and the Woolseys were great friends of my parents. He even had his own courthouse there."

"I was Judge Woolsey's law clerk when he tried many cases including his most famous — the 'Ulysses' case — and spent most of one summer in that courthouse. We took the train from New York to Springfield and then drove the rest of the way."

"Well, sir, if you looked out that courthouse window to the west, you might have seen me, or my siblings, picking blueberries, just beyond the stone wall. My parents' home was also somewhat visible from there — through the trees a bit to the right of the blueberries."

(John Munro Woolsey [1872–1945], a native of South Carolina and the first editor of the *Columbia Law Review*, had a long career as an admiralty lawyer before appointment to the Federal Bench by President Hoover. His courthouse had been the town hall of Prescott when that adjacent township was legally abolished in the 1930s to make way for the Quabbin Reservoir, and the judge had paid to relocate the historic structure to a knoll behind his home. By unanimous consent, all parties to one lengthy copyright trial agreed to adjourn the proceedings to the bucolic, hilltop atmosphere of Petersham — a town that was once the largest wheat-growing locality in the newly independent United States — while unanimously stipulating agreement to maintain the "legal fiction" of being in the sweltering, midsummer heat of downtown Manhattan.)

When Nizer and his retinue came back into the courtroom, any possibility of his continuing the film industry's abusive courtroom tactics against the government's witnesses (of which there were several more) had evaporated; Judge Dawson and I had become friends.

◆　　◆　　◆

Preemptions

One of the recurrent issues between networks and their affiliates concerned preemptions for important regional and local events. In this category we came to include our prize-winning weekly high-school quiz program — *As Schools Match Wits,* which WWLP first aired in a preempted half hour of the early evening, as well as the "Grand Ball" and related festivities surrounding the Holyoke St. Patrick's Day parade. In addition, the networks, under pressure from some affiliates for weekend baseball and other sports, tried to have it both ways — in baseball, for instance, by offering a game important to some affiliates on one weekend, and another game, important to others, on the next Saturday — and so on throughout the season, thereby keeping everyone sometimes happy. They never seemed to understand that — in New England, for instance — their several affiliates wanted the network to provide Red Sox games every weekend during the baseball season. In Dayton, their affiliates wanted the Cincinnati Reds in a similar fashion.

Some years later, when I was on the NBC Television Affiliates Board, during our periodic meetings with the NBC big shots, we tried to get the idea across, but it was often fruitless, for the network wanted the full schedule of these games for its owned stations in the major markets of New York, Chicago, Cleveland, Washington and Los Angeles and had real costs in these originations as well as other economic issues. It needed more than fitful clearances from its affiliates, in order for it not to "take a bath" in meeting the erratic and seemingly inconsistent desires of stations in 200 other markets across the country. All of this, of course, was in the simpler days when network programming was provided at known and regular hours across the country and station ownerships were limited to a practical maximum of five per legal entity.

At the affiliates' plenary meeting in Los Angeles — in 1982 — the affiliate manager from WCSH-TV in Portland, Maine, expressed the general frustration during a presentation by NBC's vice-president for sports, Art Watson, who was in the midst of a pitch for fuller clearance for NBC's next season weekend baseball schedule. "But, sir, perhaps you don't understand our situation; you like us to be strong in our markets, which means we have to do our best to carry what our viewers want. But — in New England — the Red Sox are not a ball club, they're a religion!"

At every plenary meeting of the Affiliates, some NBC big shot was sure to make a pitch for clearances of the network's weakest offerings. This always caused some soul-searching on the part of station owners. We all wanted occasional special favors of the network and so, in all fairness, we had to bear some part of the burdens of running it. At this point in our careers, WWLP accounted for about one quarter of 1 percent of the network's total average circulation, so I knew where we stood — other than whatever stature and influence the two of us were able to garner in the industry and elsewhere, we needed NBC far more than they did us. One year, the clearance pitch was particularly eloquent when one of the network's

Phil Shepardson hosted the *Wicky Wacky Cloud Club* on weekends, then graduated into hosting an award-winning high school quiz program, *As Schools Match Wits*, which ran in prime time until the FCC mandated closed-captioning for any such program.

presenters reminded us of the late Johnny Weissmuller, the one-time champion Olympic swimmer who went on to make eleven of the Tarzan movies, and was thereafter avidly sought out by his successors for advice on how to play that part. Said Johnny to one of his budding replacements: "Hmmm. Let me think. I've got it! As you swing through the jungle, don't let go of the vine!"

That high school quiz program, *As Schools Match Wits*, was always a tough one for our Sales Department, despite its continually receiving high praise in many quarters. We aired it weekly at 7:30 P.M. in what became known as the "access" period. It consisted of a quiz contest between two local high school, or prep school, teams — nothing really new in broadcasting, though the General Electric Company had something similar on the CBS network and threatened us with legal action for infringing on *their* idea. We told them to bug off — they did not own the idea of a quiz contest — and they went away. However, it was the Federal Communications Commission itself that ultimately forced the program off WWLP's air. This occurred after we had sold the station. In its continually demonstrated lack of appreciation for the unintended economic impacts of its rulings, the FCC mandated that any such origination, whether by network, syndication, or local station, should have expensive closed captioning, for the benefit of any hearing-impaired viewers. Our successors took that occasion to drop the financially unremunerative program, rather than seek a waiver so as to be able to continue a unique local service. So much for realistic regulation in the totality of the public interest. The FCC does this quite often, in its supposedly idealistic attempts to cause greater and better "service to the public."

◆ ◆ ◆

Background Noise

[KBP] One of our news photographers, Hunter Low, had worked for the Signal Corps (the photographic unit of Uncle Sam's Army that had been in operation for nearly a century as an outgrowth of General William Babcock Hazen's patronage of Mathew Brady's classic and pioneering pictures taken during the Civil War). In due course, Hunter received an offer from his former employers to return as a producer/director for the U.S. Army's series *The Big Picture*. So he left WWLP, but

Former 1st Lt. Bill Putnam speaks with his one-time commanding general, George Price Hays (who was one jeep behind him in reaching the Po River on 13 April, 1945), before the filming of the U.S. Army's Big Picture segment *The Climb to Glory* at WWLP.

remembered us when he was asked to produce a film on the famed 10th Mountain Division, entitled *The Climb to Glory*.

The Big Picture was a weekly program produced from 1951 to 1964 that was offered at no charge to television stations across the country, until it ran exclusively on ABC-TV. It included segments about a great variety of military units, and WWLP's leader was honored to be one of the talent/narrators in the film on the 10th Mountain, in which he had received several decorations for gallantry and other services.

On the appointed day, Hunter and a full crew with multiple 35 mm sound cameras returned to Provin Mountain and assembled his talent, Sergeant Ben Busch, the divisional chaplain and Bill. He planned to open Bill's segment with former 1st Lieutenant Putnam (one-time commander of Company L, 85th Mtn. Inf.) splitting logs, and looking up to intone his account of the final push out of the Appenine Mountains and into the Po Valley — in which drive Bill's company was the first Allied unit to reach the Po River. (He says that's another story.)

However, WWLP had often been bedeviled by a trap-rock quarry some two miles to the north, the operators of which would periodically set off a five-minute-long series of multiple blasts of dynamite, at unannounced intervals, in the process of pulverizing a segment of the same basaltic ridge (actually a 300-foot-thick lava flow from the Triassic age — a companion to the Palisades, across the Hudson River from New York City) on which WWLP was located, the product of which explosions was used to provide ballast for various regional highway projects as well as roadbed repairs for the Boston and Albany Railroad. The shocks and rumblings from that process could even be heard inside our studios, and we had tried (unsuccessfully) to have them do their thing when our studio was not engaged in a local event. Fortunately for our operations, the quarry crew closed down every afternoon before we began our early evening local programs, but my daytime hour was often a victim.

On this particular morning, the quarry let loose at almost the same moment that Hunter's opening cues were given to his cameramen and talent, and just as Bill started his lines, he heard the cry: "CUT! CUT! We'll have to do a retake when that noise stops." Almost immediately, however, it was realized that the quarry people had inadvertently provided a most appropriate background to a "war combat" story, for their explosions resembled distant artillery fire, and Hunter ordered his sound cameras to roll again.

◆　◆　◆

The Brothers Marek

[WLP] On the January day in 1961 that Jack Kennedy was to be inaugurated as the nation's 35th president, the City of Washington had already been blanketed with a foot of snow, from a storm which formed off the Carolinas and moved on up the East Coast, and our weatherman was predicting this disturbance would make getting around quite difficult in New England. Regardless of the weather, television coverage of the inauguration would, of course, be provided by NBC, starting with the *Today Show*, but this event was obviously of particular significance for the people of Massachusetts. The snowstorm began to arrive in our area the preceding evening and I determined that we just had to get WWLP on the air the next morning, in a timely manner, so I might as well go try to help. FCC regulations in effect at that time mandated the presence of at least one first-class licensed engineer at every broadcasting transmitter site for both radio and television.

Our regular sign-on crew consisted of two such engineers, the brothers Max and Lucian Marek, who lived in Holyoke. Given our weatherman's lugubrious forecast, I wasn't sure the Mareks would be able to make it up "the mountain" as usual; so I arose around 4:30 A.M. and started driving toward WWLP. The main roadways, while already covered with 6 to 8 inches of snow, were still negotiable in the flats, but when I came to the sustained upgrade at the Waterworks, I could see there were tracks of some vehicle ahead of me, though they were fast becoming obscured by the increasingly heavy fall of snow. My car, a newer but still sturdy Chrysler station wagon, plowed along in good form, but had to slow for a tight switchback curve near the crest of the hill. By this time, I had already passed one abandoned car and saw only rapidly disappearing footprints ahead of me through the falling snow.

When I tried regaining traction for the final upgrade, I was defeated by a deep snow drift and noticed, when I was able to back out of it to try for a second effort, that the imprint of the top of the hood of my car was in the snow. This was a sufficiently convincing sign of impossibility, so I maneuvered my car to rest beside the snow-covered other in the Water Department's parking lot and pulled out my ski poles, snowshoes and heavy parka, starting to follow those barely discernible footprints up the road toward the station. Being on frequent call for mountain rescue operations in New Hampshire's White Mountains, I always had winter mountaineering gear in the car. It was now close to 0600 and on any normal day, we would soon be going through the sign-on drill, for which the station had everything on film and audio tape. So I soldiered on for almost another mile along the crest of the ridge, following those increasingly faint footprints in the almost knee-deep snow on the road ahead of me, as time grew more and more critical. Since I held only a third-class FCC license, I did not have the legally necessary ticket to fire up our transmitter, but I felt that a phone call to someone else would give me sufficient instructions to get it going in this kind of emergency.

WWLP "just growed," as the years went on—note the horn antenna on the roof (to pick up and monitor the WRLP signal). A regional fire lookout can be seen over the station logo (1958).

At last I was able to burst in the station door, where everything was suddenly bright and warm. My worst fears had been abolished by the foresight and determined loyalty of Max and Lou, who had also anticipated difficult going, whose footsteps I had been following and who promptly offered me a cup of hot coffee. WWLP was, moreover, the only station receivable in our area that did sign on as usual that day—some did not make it on the air until late afternoon.

By the way, Lucian, the late elder brother, whose unforgettable laugh often resounded throughout the building, was frequently chairman of the National Association of Broadcast Employees and Technicians (NABET) Local 13. Max was the preferred polka partner for Kitty, hurtling her wildly about the floor at company events. It was also these two who took it on themselves to "pull in the sweeps" on our station's picture, thus providing a suitable black border to our live coverage of my father's funeral in late 1972.

5

Building a Local Audience

The Bal de Tête

[KBP] Given our unforgettable need for overcoming the "lack of UHF receivers" problem, we decided early on to cover every significant local event we could possibly get to, and thus we needed remote origination capability, which would have to include no less than two cameras, all the associated audio and control equipment and a portable microwave link — a transmitter unit that would travel with the truck. So Bill and George started scrounging around for what Roland Filiault said we could afford, and by late in 1955 had obtained two Dumont cameras, a Raytheon microwave and some GE audio and control equipment. Jim Ferguson's staff had promoted a sizeable Dodge van on some kind of swap advertising deal. The only item in it all that I'm sure everyone thoroughly understood how to operate was that truck. Bill and George had built a special platform for the microwave receiver at the 300-foot level of our tower, at which the receiving dish could be panned and tilted from down in the control room.

Considerably more than parenthetic to everything Springfield Television accomplished was Roland's ability to come up with the money for almost any capital outlay we really needed. A one-time employee of the IRS and a superb money manager he would regularly invest whatever means we had available in the overnight funds market and squirrel away a few CDs in anticipation of whatever Bill and George might be planning for the future, so he could (though often loudly grumbling) come through in the clutch. Roland was also a founding director of the Institute for Broadcast Financial Management. Once, however, when Bill had bought some roses to enhance the station's front door appearance, Roland's deputy, Peggy McGee, almost had a seizure before she read the full text of an invoice for a half-dozen "Chrysler Imperials."

Some of the WWLP technical staff in 1980: Lou Chenevert, a visiting electronics salesman, our fancy Universal Zoomar lens, Al Hedin, Max Marek, Thurston Thompson.

However, our leader unfortunately decided to give the station's new toy a baptism by fire at a fund-raising event — where all the paying participants were required to wear some unique headgear — in support of the Springfield Symphony Orchestra. This grand affair was to be held at the Highland Hotel, then Springfield's premier downtown eatery — but later a victim of urban renewal — so George and the engineers "cased the joint" for everything we needed, including sufficient elevation for the microwave link to clear intervening buildings and get a line-of-sight to the mountain and a "clean" source of electric power. I (who had a background including many amateur theatricals and had already done a few studio fashion shows for the station) was to introduce and narrate the affair, so we all arrived on the scene early enough to get everything set up appropriately and have a bite of the Highland's famous lobster dinner (See appendix A).

In the set-up process, Bill had been handed a heavy wire and asked

Bowling show remote; the ceiling had to be lifted for cameraman Al Hedin to stand erect.

to take one end of it from the truck to inside the building and attach it to some piece of plumbing, so the truck would have an effective ground. What ensued should have been a wake-up warning, for when Bill approached a sink in the hotel's dishwashing area, the #6 copper wire accidentally brushed against the polished steel metal and a three-inch length of wire promptly welded itself to the hotel — where it stayed until the famous old eatery was torn down a few years later.

Producer/director George Mitchell and audioman Lou Marek at the switcher during a remote telecast of *At Home with Kitty*.

(The saga of the Highland Hotel merits a story of its own, for it was the premier eatery between the major cities of Boston and New York. At this stage of its ownership, the management consisted of the key personnel from the NordDeutscher Lloyd liner *Kronprincessin Cecelie*, which had been interned at Bar Harbor and then Boston at the outbreak of the World War in late summer of 1914.)

What none of the engineers appreciated at the time was that the portable synchronizing generator (the item which kept the 525 lines of an analog television picture in coordinated alignment) was not functioning as it should; and though they felt the truck was finally sufficiently grounded, something still wasn't quite right. Across Western Massachusetts and much of northern Connecticut, including the homes of most of the community's movers and shakers, television receivers were all but unanimously askew. In our first great attempt at impressing the key local sponsors — or at least their wives — we had flunked. The worst part of the

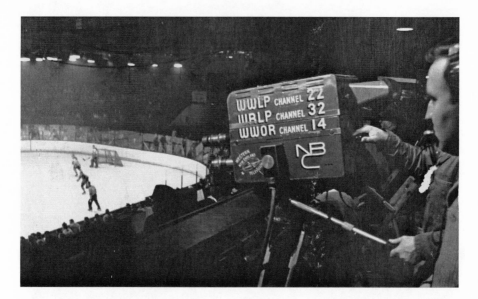

WWLP covered bowling contests, football and hockey games — and elephant walks — at or near the Eastern States Colosseum.

disaster for us was the realization that all the ladies involved had gone to particularly great pains in arranging their head gear because of the television coverage they had been promised.

Once the engineers mastered the quirks of its synchronizing generator, this Dodge van and its mostly Dumont equipment were very profitably used for many local remote telecasts, as well as NBC originations that were often sponsored by RCA and General Motors. The engineers also found a practical use for Bill's climbing ropes — hauling microwave gear up onto numerous rooftops in the Springfield area.

◆   ◆   ◆

My First Show

One Sunday evening in July of 1954, I got a phone call at home from the station's program director, "Uncle Miltie" Slater, telling me that I would have to do the cooking show early tomorrow afternoon, as the young lady he had hired for the job had just called in sick. (In fact, Mary Lou never came back; her "shrink" had told her the pressure of live television was too much for her.) At first, I told Slater I simply could not do it, as I had never been able to watch the program — I was working on radio station traffic and handling Bill's secretarial work in the downtown offices at WSPR and the studio was eight miles away, up on the mountain in Agawam. He cajoled me for a while because I was also rather miffed, having asked for the job in the first place, and having been told by him that I was unsuitable for the program he planned, since I wanted to do a lot to appeal to homemakers rather than the normal industry-standard cooking show. To this day (more than 25 years after my last show) I still meet many adults who recall being told by their parents to go watch Channel 22's *At Home with Kitty*, it not being a racy soap opera. I guess I became an electronic babysitter for thousands.

Needless to say, Slater finally convinced me, and after I hung up with him, I started reviewing my home inventory of what would be easy

Director Wayne Henry Latham with Kitty and Tom Colton.

to put together that I could be sure of not messing up. Little did I know the pitfall I would encounter the next day. For the main event of the show, I finally selected a sponge cake with chocolate whipped-cream frosting. I called a couple of my friends for moral support, one of whom offered me the use of some plastic bowls and her electric blender, to prepare the whipped cream. Even in those early days of television, it was established that any cooking show should have visible, right at the start, [A] the finished product, ready to eat; [B] a tray holding the various raw ingredients; and [C] a display of the bowls and other utensils needed for preparing the recipe.

After settling things with Slater, I prepared the finished sponge cake at home that very evening and brought it to the mountain in the morning with everything else I felt I would need. I talked it all over with the producer/director, Wayne Henry Latham, another asset gleaned from WSPR, and barely had the opportunity to brush my hair before it was time to start the program. Besides being a longtime member of Springfield's Liquor License Commission, Wayne had a resonant baritone voice that made him a "must" as the off-camera master of ceremonies at every classy public event in greater Springfield, and he also had a deep knowledge of show biz. From my conversation with him I figured that all I had to do was prepare the recipe, his job was to get the video and audio together, so I would not have to worry about that. Then, when the lights came on our studio cameras, I carefully cut the sponge cake in half, lengthwise, and everything seemed to be going so well that I began to relax.

Plastic bowls were quite new in 1954 and as I was whipping the cream, I tipped it slightly so as to let it be seen by one of the cameras. Then, when I removed the beater to better show the contents, the bowl, being quite slick, slid up out of my hands and fell, kersplat, upside down, onto the studio floor. I was stunned and (very rarely in my life) at a loss for words. Just then, one of the cameramen stage-whispered "Kitty!" and I looked up, thinking he was going to offer me some help out of this disaster. "Wayne says he would like to lick the bowl." I stared into the camera and said, "Well, if I had whipped cream, this is what I would do next," which brought more giggles from behind the cameras. Finally, the show ended. I have never been more grateful for the end of any television program, but my miseries were only beginning. Back upstairs in our diminutive office, Bill tried to buck up my spirits, but I soon had to leave for home.

Hostess Kitty has a few words for the cameraman before opening her daily show.

As I shopped for groceries, one of my friends approached me in the store and confided that earlier that day he had seen one of the funniest incidents ever on television and it was on our station's cooking show. My embarrassment was not yet over.

As I was preparing dinner at home, the phone rang; it was the friend who had loaned me the blender.

"What color was that dress you had on today?"

"Red and white checked. Why? What's wrong?"

"It made you look fat."

The innocent dress was never seen again.

Another phone call told me that I should not wear my hair pulled back into a "George Washington" bow — it made my ears stick out. After a few more calls of that nature, I decided I did not have the time, nor did the station have the facilities, for me to try to be glamorous; I would either be myself or forget all about being on the air. My children continued to have a difficult time understanding why I could not be as well turned-out as

Dinah Shore, but no local station, particularly one in the UHF band, could afford extensive wardrobe, make-up or hairdo people.

Some of My Favorite Guests

As my "cooking" show gradually expanded to include ever more news and information, I interviewed many of the Kennedy political family and determined that the matriarchal Rose was the most effective presenter in her family. In 1957, she and her two daughters came to Springfield to do some politicking for Jack, who was then seeking reelection to the United States Senate. All the local news media had been alerted as to where there would be interviews available, beginning at 4:00 P.M., so I arrived early with our cameraman, but still had to struggle my way to the front of quite a crowd; every radio station for 80 miles around seemed to be represented. Mrs. Kennedy took immediate charge, asking for silence — and getting it. She then divided the milling crowd of reporters into three sections — print, radio and television, and said she would start with TV — which meant me.

I promptly moved up next to her, introducing myself with microphone in hand, while she straightened her long, white, kid gloves, a small pillbox hat and her black dress as we both waited for the camera light to come on.

"Kitty! Ask me about John as a baby."

I did as asked, and for the next seven minutes did not have to utter another word. She took over and even spotted the wind-up cues — just like a real pro.

I really enjoyed my frequent interviews with the Boston Pops legendary conductor, Arthur Fiedler (1894–1980). He would stop by the mountain almost every year, on his way to Tanglewood for the Pops summer series in the Berkshires. As honorary chief of the Boston Fire Department, he loved excitement and brought that spirit with him wherever he went. His summer concerts at Lenox were always sellouts, with people picnicking on the extensive lawn outside the music shell. He was a very vibrant man, regaling an audience with many anecdotes of his upbringing in Austria (though he was born in America) and of interesting musical episodes, and other stories which brought much of that personal zest to his appearances. I always managed to find time for him, even when one of his staff would call me at the "last possible" moment, perhaps as he was driving up to the station.

I interviewed many budding politicians, as well as their wives, since the spouses, merely by their appearance and manner, often spoke volumes about the candidates themselves, and what they were like as human beings. One very interesting such guest was Rosalynn Carter (Mrs. James Earl, Jr). I asked her what had convinced her husband to seek the office of president.

"Well, Kitty," she drawled in her charming Georgia accent, "when we lived in the governor's mansion in Atlanta, a great many famous people would come by for a visit, and after I had met quite a few of them, one night I told Jimmy; 'You're a lot smarter than most of those men, Jimmy; you ought to run for President.'" I thought she was a lovely and charming person, and agreed with her reasoning about her husband, an opinion that has only been reinforced by the nation's experience with Mr. Carter's successors.

Jimmy Carter needed at least 15 percent of the Massachusetts Democratic Convention delegate support (which was being held in Springfield that year) in order to qualify for a place on the Massachusetts primary ballot. So Bill and I both talked with our friend Eddie Boland, urging him to corral the necessary delegate votes. Later I drove Mr. Carter down to the airport after our interview, and enjoyed being his chauffeur, even briefly; he was a very gracious guest — and did quite well in the subsequent primary vote, too.

Barbara Eden was a glamorous guest with a lovely sense of humor, so she was a fun interview. But after I wrapped up her segment, which we taped on a carpet-covered riser for a rerun presentation later, and was

talking my way through a commercial — the video of which was on film —
as I walked slowly over to the studio kitchen for the next segment of the
show, I heard a muffled shriek behind me. The cameramen and the boom
mike operator immediately stopped following me so they could run to Ms.
Eden's aid. It seemed that in trying to get up and quietly exit the studio,
she had tipped back in her chair and fallen onto the carpet in considerable
disarray, but still with very good humor. Rushing to the rescue of the
glamorous star of *I Dream of Jeannie* and the famous Bob Hope USO
shows was much more important for the male studio crew than moving
the mike or making my program look good. After all, she was a "once-
in-a-lifetime" visitor, and they had to deal with me every day of the week.

Once I actually tried to be glamorous. The opportunity came when
I was interviewing Gig Young, who was visiting at the Storrowton Music
Tent. For this interview, I tried out a pair of false eyelashes that were sup-
posed to make me as attractive as Miss Eden. But there was a problem.
The studio air conditioner could not be operated while we were live,
because it caused a low rumble in the audio; so, during the summers, we

ran it at full blast prior to any
studio show and then shut it off
during the actual telecast time.
Therefore, the studio got increasingly warm as any interview pro-
gressed, and on this occasion my
"glamorous" new eyelashes started
to slip out of place. Periodically,
I would brush them back, in
what I hoped was appearing as a
casual gesture, until finally one
was dangling in front of my nose
and could no longer be toler-
ated. I pulled them both off and
tossed the ersatz eyelashes onto
the coffee table, telling my movie
star guest that "I guess that kind
of glamour is not for me." He
laughed at the event and thanked
me for my candor.

As time went on, I got to

**Springfield Television's hostess (and later
president) did real well without trying
for artificial glamour.**

interview quite a number of famous show business people, most of whom were the same off camera as on, and most of whom I found to be genuinely kind and helpful. My older son, Rick, was a great fan of singer Keely Smith, the sometime wife of trumpeter Louis Prima (1910–1978), and had a huge stack of her records, though he had never been able to take in one of her live performances. One day, in preparing for an interview with her, I mentioned my son's interest, and that he was then away at Boston University. Some weeks later, when she was performing at a nightclub in the Boston area, she looked up Rick's address and sent him two tickets so he and a friend could have front row seats at her show — all on the house.

◆   ◆   ◆

A Big Sale

Jim Ferguson, our general sales manager, and another acquisition from WSPR, could sell ice cubes to Eskimos, and had managed to get WWLP on the air in a completely sold-out condition. Of course, when the realization that we had almost no audience hit the offices of those sponsors, many of them drifted away. We shall always remember those few who stayed with us, in a gesture of encouragement for what they knew we were trying to do in and for our community — a list that would always be headed by Arthur Joseph Boyer, a small-time home builder and plumbing contractor (who could only afford one ten-second station ID per week) and include Bob Samble, owner of a local laundry (who sponsored a late Friday evening weather forecast), and Howard J. Cadwell, the CEO of Western Massachusetts Electric Company, who arranged for his firm to buy a 15-minute evening interview program every weeknight, a paid sponsorship that we signed on with and was almost equal to our monthly electric bill. WMECo's contribution to our ultimate survival was enormous! Reddy Kilowatt furnished not only the talent and the content of interesting interviews with local personalities, but paid for the prime time slot at our published rates. Their program idea and slogan — "Western Massachusetts is the world's *best* place in which to live, work and play" — spread across the nation, and now we even watch a utility-sponsored, western version of this concept in Arizona. For ten years, we billed WMECo almost the same amount every month as they billed us. To this day, we think nice

A singing trio as guests on *Western Massachusetts Highlites*.

thoughts about its late chairman, Mr. Cadwell. Several years later, under his leadership, WMECo became the critical organizational component of Northeast Utilities.

When Jim's staff finally landed a local beer distributor, with a full sponsorship of Lloyd Bridges' *Sea Hunt*, he decided we needed to throw a party for the beer deliverymen. This was before the days of videotape and I was scheduled to deliver a live commercial in the studio shortly after 5 P.M. Ferguson wanted me to be at the Oaks Hotel on the far side of town to greet everyone before 6:00; and that afternoon — our semi-pro weatherman's assertions to the contrary notwithstanding — it started to snow. I would have loved to be able to use the one-inch (and smaller) video-tape apparatus that became so common later, though it was still a dream in the minds of equipment makers (mostly Japanese). In due course, however, WWLP was to be among the first stations in the country to install this equipment.

Kitty and Aunt Jemima visiting in the studio kitchen.

The commercial went well — I have a good gift of gab and excellent short-term memory, so I could read a commercial script a couple of times, hold up a product, and then deliver the lines while looking straight into the camera. Then I ran to the ladies' room, put on my party dress and went out to my car, now covered with two inches of new snow. Here I was, on top of a snowy mountain, alone, in a party outfit, complete with white gloves, and rapidly becoming late for Jim's gathering. Everyone else — the entire sales crew, Bill, George and Jim — were already downtown hoisting a few. So I did what I had to do — brushed my car's windshield free of snow and started down the hill.

I still don't know what happened, but after "it" was over, my car had gone off the road, narrowly missing a few trees, and was stuck in some thorny bushes twenty yards into the forest. What to do?

Kitty making a pitch for her first sponsor — White House Coffee.

I climbed out of the undamaged but firmly stuck car, contemplating a miserable hike back up the slippery road to the station, where I knew that Roland Filiault was still at work. He'd be able to get me to my new assignment as station hostess. But fortunately, dear Roland was already on the way down, and stopped when he saw my bedraggled self trying to struggle with high heels through several inches of slippery snow back uphill to the station.

He rolled down the window. "Where's your car, Kathryn?"

"Down there! Can't you see it?" I pointed into the forest.

"Nope. I guess you'll want a ride downtown?"

"If you please," I climbed in, and Roland — one of the best drivers I have ever known — took off as if there were no raging snowstorm and soon delivered my worried and shook-up self to the appointed spot.

"Mother! Where the hell have you been?" was Bill's only greeting, as the gentlemanly Roland escorted me into the hotel.

"My car went off the road."

"All by itself," the unsympathetic brute remarked. "Well, get over here and act like you need a Budweiser." He was "all kindness" and ignored my torn stockings, water-stained gloves, messed-up hairdo and wet, snow-streaked shoes, very much in a hurry for me to charm Jim's big-spending clients.

"I've got to go to the ladies' room and tidy up a bit."

"You look wonderful, Mother. I've got a long tow chain; Roland and I will take care of your car later."

I went to the ladies' room anyway, but only after giving him the kind of look he deserved. As for my poor car, when the party broke up a couple of hours later, Bill, Roland and I drove back up to the scene of the event and the two men looked down into the woods to where my pale green two-door Ford station wagon was barely visible through the still falling snow. "It's down there, you say?"

"Yep! Can't you see it?"

"Yeah, sorta. How in hell did you manage to miss all those trees? Guess we'll have to get a wrecker up here to fetch it out of that pucker-brush. We'll take you home, now, Mother dear, and I'll come fetch you in the morning."

His earlier bravado had vanished, and I still like to think it was awe at my skill in avoiding the bigger trees while getting so far into the forest.

Sharing an office with William had its occasional benefits. Even back at the chamber of commerce, I had instructed my children to call me at work as soon as they were home from school. Karen, the older, would dutifully dial in, and sometimes — if I was occupied — Bill would answer the phone at my desk in our office.

"Hello...."

"Mother?"

"I'm not your mother; she's down the hall." So he would often yell, "Hey, Mother, your daughter's on the horn."

The name stuck — in time the broadcast industry trade press reporters picked it up — and almost 60 years later, he still occasionally calls me "Mother" (among other names), though my elder daughter now has grandchildren.

◆ ◆ ◆

A Short (Very) Ski Trip

After one heavy snowstorm, we decided to do a ski program on the slopes in front of the station. I, of course, picked my best "ski bunny" outfit, so I could look professional. Sun shining brightly on the new snow,

I climbed up the small knoll in front of WWLP and started to get in place. Bill (who very correctly doubted my ability to ski) brought some snowshoes for me to try out, and a real ski instructor was standing by to demonstrate. Once I was "miked," Bill finally strapped my feet into the snowshoes and I intoned "Good afternoon. Welcome to the great outdoors ..." and took one step backward, only to fall embarrassingly on my backside. No one had told me that snow shoes only go forward. I picked myself up (with help from Bill, who materialized from off-camera), brushed myself off and continued with the show. Living in a suburban town and meeting people at the local grocery store has both advantages and disadvantages. On my way home that evening, I stopped to buy groceries and was complimented on my dexterity (or lack thereof) by several "friends" who had caught the show.

(A few years later, Bill actually tried getting me to ski. We were visiting KSTU, in Salt Lake City, and had the weekend free, so he convinced

A snowbunny on Provin Mountain.

me to go with him up to Park City, then being developed, and try a few hours "on the boards." But, unfortunately, I really am a dyed-in-the-wool snow bunny, and neither one of us enjoyed his attempts to get me to be happy navigating even one of the "green circle" slopes.)

Thanksgiving

For some years, I had a local group of eleven individually-owned grocery stores as sponsors for a 20-minute segment every Thursday, and I tried to incorporate their weekly specials whenever possible. One year, I decided to do a traditional Thanksgiving Dinner (for ten) on Wednesday, because the Macy's Fifth Avenue Parade on NBC preempted my time slot on Thanksgiving Day. I invited a couple of the engineers and several of the office staff to join me in the studio, sit down and eat the dinner — on the air. After spending the morning in my studio kitchen getting every-thing ready, I thought things were going quite well and looked forward to an interesting program. Then the visiting staff members came in and took their places around the impromptu dining table. I had planned to open this show holding my fresh-from-the-oven Waybest turkey. At 12:59:30 I got the one-half-minute cue, then opened the oven door to take out the turkey, and finally turned to face the cameras. At the moment I turned, the 16-pound entree suddenly developed a mind of its own. The bird slid from the platter, slithered across the studio floor and came to rest in a far corner. Amid muffled giggling from my assembled "guests," I stared down the scoffers, put the empty platter on the table and started what I now feared was to be an hour-long ordeal. As was usual practice in cooking shows, we had prepared a second bird, which was on stand-by, precooked and already partially sliced, so the show could go on, minus the opening guest star.

However, there was a minor sequel. I had carefully placed several strips of salt pork across the turkeys' bodies, a new recipe to provide bast-ing while the bird was in the oven, and mentioned that my sponsors all carried the Waybest turkeys, for those who wished to follow the recipe. Unfortunately, I had neglected to inform the group of stores about the basting idea, and I caught a lot of flak when several of them ran out of salt pork that afternoon. "Please tell us, Kitty, next time you're going to plug something we don't normally keep in reserve stock."

Storrowton Music Tent

Every summer, many folks in western Massachusetts looked forward to the live shows put on by the local impressario, Wally Beach, at the Storrowton Music Tent (summer theater) on the grounds of the Eastern States Exposition in West Springfield. At my suggestion, WWLP televised a half-hour interview segment on opening night in the 7:30 P.M. "access period"—and one year that event featured dancer Bobby Van, singer and Broadway star Patricia Morrison, and Hollywood star, Mickey Rooney. My favorite co-host was our jack-of-all-trades and sports director (after Burleigh Brown opted to work at WRLP) Roland Jacobs. One year, as airtime approached, I had already spoken with Van, being careful—as usual—to determine if there were any topics that were utterly taboo, or that the guest wished to have me bring out. Rollie held a similar conversation with Morrison, but there was no sign of Rooney, and the show had to start live at 7:30. The Van interview went well and then the genial Rollie interviewed Morrison equally smoothly. Finally, I heard the familiar phrase, "... *and now back to Kitty* ..." from Rollie. But there was still no Mickey Rooney—despite several requests, he had refused to leave his dressing room.

I feared that I had the remaining eight minutes to fill and started with comments on the beautiful weather, the overflow crowd and what a great show it was going to be—all the time wondering "Where is he?" Just then, I saw my missing guest running toward the stage, and as he passed one of the cameramen, he asked; "What's her name?" Upon being informed, he rushed into camera and microphone range, smiling broadly, and exclaimed, "Hi, Kitty!" as if we were old friends. Despite the lack of preparation, the interview went smoothly. Later, I learned that he was going through a number of personal problems, which explained his unusual behavior, but he was a real pro.

Wally (actually Wallrath) Beach was an avid show biz promoter, and he managed to induce quite a number of big-time stars to come and perform for his various ventures. But one of his early promotions included a trio of singers who were just starting out in 1961, Mary Travers, Paul Stookey and Peter Yarrow — "Peter, Paul and Mary." Bill and I heard them one evening at Wally's Coffee House in downtown Springfield, and the next day, they did an early version of their most famous hit, "Blowin' in the Wind," at our studios for me.

Wladziu Valentino Liberace (1919–1987) — small wonder he used his last name in show biz — was born in Milwaukee of an immigrant Polish mother and an immigrant Italian father and had been playing the piano from the age of four. He was another of Wally's frequent performers and he also loved to cook, Italian-style. When he was appearing at the Storrowton Music Tent, he would come up to visit with me on the air in the afternoon and he always stayed at the home of the late Ann Corio (star of *This Was Burlesque* and the prime attraction at Bill's Harvard freshman class "blowout" in 1941) and her manager/husband, Mike Ianucci, in nearby Suffield, Connecticut. During every week he was on stage, I was always invited down to Ann's home for a spaghetti dinner of an evening, which Liberace prepared for his hosts. He was a warm and entertaining guest — invariably a sellout performer — and he never failed to make those who appeared with him feel comfortable.

Martha Ray (1916–1994), self-styled as "Big Mouth," was just as funny and warm off-stage as when actually performing, but Milton Berle (1908–2002), her occasional co-host and NBC television's earliest big star performer, was something else. He was best on the "borscht circuit" and was particularly noted, if not infamous, for upstaging anyone who appeared with him. But despite some of his failings, NBC's "Uncle Miltie" invariably adhered to his

Kitty, impresario Wally Beach, and Mike Ianucci at the Storrowton Music Tent.

Kitty dressed for the occasion when interviewing Liberace.

most famous line — "Always Leave 'Em Laughing." I really liked the genuinely friendly Ms. Ray, who ended her TV career doing commercials for
Polident, but I was always on guard when talking with Berle, who made
me feel that it was beneath him to visit a non-network television studio.

Kitty after an interview with Jack Benny.

Stepping Out with Babe

In mid–September of 1970, before any of my children had gone away to college, we were doing my regular show from the grounds of the Eastern States Exposition (the Big E) when my then producer/director, Ron Langevin, lined up a guest who had a bunch of show animals and asked Ron if I would be up to going for a ride on an ostrich. Ron said, "Sure!" A few minutes before show time, Ron came over to tell me that the ostrich

Period costume docents from Colonial Sturbridge Village.

was acting up that day and the guest was now suggesting that it might be better for me to have his elephant walk over me. This was a different twist, but I, still thinking it all a joke, said, "Of course," and turned to my first guest, as it was now almost time to sign on the program.

As soon as I was engaged in my opening on-the-air patter, out of the corner of my eye, I could see two of the engineers removing some padding blankets from the remote truck, while behind them a huge, grey elephant was placidly approaching. Soon I was introducing the trainer, who promptly assured me that Babe did not weigh any more than three tons, adding, "Kitty, you don't have to be *very* brave; Babe has this routine pretty well figured out by now and she's only stepped on a couple of people in her lifetime."

With that cheerful news, I lay down on the padded blankets, feeling pretty stupid — but somehow not frightened. Then, when Babe's big left front foot was raised over my midriff, dropping sawdust and dirt onto me, I heard the trainer say, "No, No, Babe! That's the wrong foot! Bring it back and start over again." Babe gave a snort in acknowledgment; her dinner plate-sized left front foot was returned and her right front foot then went clear of my nose, soon followed by her right hind foot. Then the trainer reached down to help me to my feet — and the show went on. I never saw the out-of-sorts, temperamental ostrich.

When I drove home a couple of hours later, my children were lined up on the back porch with varying degrees of concern on their faces. The eldest, Karen, spoke up: "Mother! You're nuts! Did you really have an elephant walk over you?" It had been all over the Longmeadow School system. The Big E people used that bit in their ads for a decade thereafter, and I must be one of the few people in the world who knows what the bottom of an elephant's foot looks like, close up.

◆ ◆ ◆

A Cooking Aftermath

All kinds of food companies employed traveling demonstrators to call on people like me for interviews. For example, I interviewed several very competent and well-spoken Aunt Jemimas, one of whom told me, after the show was concluded for the day, that she was the senior of several such ladies employed by the Quaker Oats Company, and who were now, unfortunately, all about to lose their jobs because what they did was apparently "categorically denigrating to blacks." I see now (many years later) that this unfortunate "taboo" has been somewhat relaxed, and that Aunt Jemima and Uncle Ben are back on the interview circuit.

Another day my producer had scheduled a young lady from the Swiss Cheese Foundation who flew up from New York just for the interview. On camera she prepared a delightful Gruyère fondue, but then I had to pause for a filmed commercial and she confided that she had to hurry back to the airport because her plane was due to leave in less than an hour. I wished her well and did the other interviews we had scheduled in the living room set, while she took her fancy, professional fondue pot and quietly left the studio kitchen.

When I came out of the studio, at the end of the hour, Bill and Roland were out in the hallway wielding mops — there had obviously been some kind of flood. So I tiptoed across the soggy hallway carpet and started to run upstairs to our office. Then it struck me; I knew what might have caused the flood, so I turned around and told them, "I bet it's that hot fondue. My guest must have poured it down the toilet before leaving the building, so she could go home with a clean pot; and I'm sure it congealed into a lump when it hit the cold water."

I never heard the end of that interview, because the building's throne rooms were perforce all closed and Bill had to spend the rest of the afternoon working with a pick and shovel to open up and clear the drain outside the building, just before it entered the septic tank.

Encountering the Big City Labor Unions

To add some spice to my daily "cooking" show, I decided to go to New York twice a year — starting in the mid–1960s — to cover the spring and the fall fashion shows, where one could take in the various new styles that would be in the stores for the next season. This "press week" was a preview, started originally for newspapers, then broadened to allow radio commentators, and finally, with time, even television people like me were invited by the grand doyenne of American fashion, the late Eleanor Lambert, originator of the concept.

Miss Lambert was an utterly unique person, by any use of the word. Born the daughter of an Indiana circus advance man, she migrated to New York and, at the press week activities, which she initiated in 1943, she was very much in charge. Paris, the prior world capital of fashion, was then under restrictive German occupation and she had been quick to seize the opportunity this presented. The equipment we used for the filming was bulky and heavy, and my favorite station cameraman, Freddie Speckels, and I stayed at the Waldorf (where our stations had a due bill) while Eleanor's events were always held either at the Pierre or the Plaza.

One day, trying to get from one hotel to another, after a couple of empty cabs had ignored us, I realized that they probably did not want to take all of Freddie's gear, which he had piled on the sidewalk. So, I told him to step away from me inside the hotel and, sure enough, I got the very next cab. When the cabbie was stopped, I called Freddie out to join me.

Another day, as we were setting up for one of the luncheon shows and Freddie was testing the AC outlet for his lights, he was accosted by a big, burly man who told him, rather nastily, that he could not plug in there, as he was not a union cameraman. I came over and argued equally unsuccessfully with this man, but he was both very big and very adamant. Eleanor came by and I explained our unfortunate predicament. She then marched over to the bullying protestor and, looking up at him, straight in the eye, very calmly but very firmly told him that he had nothing to say about the out-of-town press (or television) people and that what my cameraman did was none of his business. And the show went on.

Miss Lambert had been through this sort of issue before. Her job was to promote the fashions and when newspaper people objected to radio people being there, she had gone through a similar argument. Then, when television came along, and others objected to our lights and equipment, she stood her ground — all 5 feet 2 inches of her.

For me to show fall fashions in the spring or early summer (July) was futile, so I saved Freddie's film (later videotape) until the very end of summer, and did similarly with the summer fashions, which we filmed in January. After she graduated from college, my elder daughter, Karen, accompanied me occasionally, and, with Eleanor's help, then found a job in the New York fashion industry.

Some years later, when I was arranging a dinner program in Boston for the American Women in Radio and Television, two men I had never met before came up and asked me if I would like to have a young lady sing for the gathering. I wondered less about her talent than if I was about to get into another tiff with some big city union, so I stalled them until I could be more sure of understanding whatever argument I might be about to encounter.

WWLP even interviewed the competition — Kitty talks with Ginger from ABC's *Gilligan's Island.*

Kitty interviews the stars of CBS's *Gunsmoke*—Dennis Weaver, Miss Kitty and Doc.

I already had a very tight program schedule, but finally, after they almost begged me to let my group of women broadcasters hear her sing, I agreed, but said that the only open time would be during our dessert. So this young lady sang one of the current pop songs — and was good — very good, I had to admit. Six months later Barbra Streisand was the star of *Funny Girl* on Broadway.

Those trips to the big city for fashion reporting had an interesting side effect, once my elder daughter started attending with me. As she wrote to Bill some forty years later:

> My mother was as amazing back then as she is now! Growing up with a "famous" TV personality had its perks, as well as the continual drawback of having to behave ourselves. Her offspring could get in free to the Eastern States Exposition (ostensibly, I am sure, to help out with her show) and I'm sure there were more such perks, though we knew you tended to frown on our taking advantage of such freebies. But, as a teenager, I used

to get embarrassed when going shopping on Main Street to Steiger's or Forbes & Wallace, as many people would stop my mother on the street and tell her how great her show was the day before, or the week before. I often kept several paces behind her as I was embarrassed to get introduced or talk to these people.

During my senior year in high school, she had my whole class on her show to dance the sock hop that was popular at that time, but I feared that the one thing which stood out on TV were my size 10 white buck shoes! But, having mother working was a plus during my junior year when I could smoke in my room and blow the smoke out the window. I don't think she knew that I smoked until I was in my twenties.

To me one of the most important aspects of having a famous mother came when I was in my mid–twenties and worked for Eleanor Lambert. During those twice a year shows, one of them just after Thanksgiving, when the radio and television editors would come to the Plaza Hotel in New York to attend Press Week, I was able to enjoy quality time with my mother, even though I was supposedly working for Estee Lauder. One day we went out to Connecticut to visit the homes of several famous fashion designers: Adele Simpson, Bill Blass, Jerry Silverman, etc. And once we visited Helena Rubenstein at her apartment in N.Y. That was real privilege and quite amazing; she was then in her eighties, short with slick, black hair pulled back in a bun and wearing a brilliant red dress with lots of jewelry — very impressive at my young age, just out of college.

◆　◆　◆

A Christmas Story

One of my most consistent sponsors was the late Forbes and Wallace department store, which ultimately became a victim of the mall mania that has overwhelmed North America in the last half-century. It had been an eight-story downtown Springfield fixture for several generations, and both Bill and I had developed personal relationships with the leading members of the Wallace family (Forbes having been bought out early on).

Indeed, one of Bill's editorials dealt with the false reasoning of one mayor of Springfield who campaigned for reelection, in part, anyhow, on the basis of his having denied city trash pick-up service to Forbes and Wallace, thus mandating that they engage a private service — at a cost which was necessarily passed on to their customers, who were also his constituents. (He lost!) Anyhow, Forbes and Wallace bought a half-hour once a week for an early evening program during the several-week run-up to

Christmas in 1959, and asked that I devote that time to reading a Christmas story to my two younger children, Morgan and Erica, then aged five and three, who were to be seated near me on small chairs.

As I started my story one evening, Morgan commenced to fidget, getting up and moving his chair as I was reading, while Erica kept steady — she was obviously prepping at an early age for her subsequent career — but not that little boy-devil. Twice, I had to say: "Please, Morgan, sit down and be still."

Then he got up and started to pester Erica again. I continued to be calm as he became more and more annoying, pestering his younger sister repeatedly, and I had to interrupt the story to command his obedience. Finally I'd had enough and slammed the book down: "Morgan Andrew Broman, turn around and SIT DOWN!" in my exasperated, parental voice.

Kitty's 1958 Christmas Eve reading program. Morgan (age 4) and Erica (age 2).

He did. The use of any child's full name was an unmistakable sign of more than exasperation — if absolute obedience did not follow immediately, the consequences could be serious.

The station's switchboard did light up, but not as I had feared, with calls about my maternal shortcomings, but with praise from numerous other mothers — and not a few fathers — for my disciplinary firmness.

Bill's Birthday

After we built WRLP in Winchester, New Hampshire, in 1957, we gave it our best effort, and periodically I would originate my program from the studio on Gun Hill, with the satellite station's feed being carried on WWLP. For this periodic effort, Bill would pick me up for the more than hour-long drive north and — in those pre-interstate highway days —

Mount Snow program, originating from the Dumont camera-equipped studio of WRLP; Ralph Jay at camera on left.

we'd have a long period of quiet in which to draft a few of his editorials, talk about station personnel issues, and plan future events. After doing my studio show (with two more Dumont cameras), for which Wallace Green, the WRLP deputy station manager, rounded up guests for, Bill and I would have another hour-long quiet period for the drive back south. Upon occasion, Bill would have sufficient other business matters to attend to that we would be late and have to stop for a bite of dinner on our trip home. There were several quality eateries along the way, and as we passed them all quite often, he and I would frequently speculate on the ambience (or lack of same), the menu, etc. of each.

On one such occasion, in late October of 1958 (William is a Scorpio to my Aquarius), I had been importuned by Lou Marek and others to see if we could arrange a surprise birthday party for "our leader." So I agreed to stall things on the drive south from WRLP so that we'd have to stop for dinner en route, and the sales department worked out a trade deal with the Wayside Inn on Route 5 in West Springfield. In my conspiracy with Lou, I had agreed that I would try to get Bill there around 6:30, so he was arranging for anyone who wanted to join us to be there a little before then.

There was a large number of quite passable restaurants along our route and as we passed the Northfield Inn, Bill inquired about stopping there and I invented some reason to demur. Then we got to Whately, and he asked, ""I've heard a lot about the political gatherings at the Whately Inn, Mother. Let's go in there and check it out." Again I was forced to demur, and invented some other reason that sounded valid to me. We continued on past the Wiggins Tavern in the center of Northampton and the Yankee Pedlar in Holyoke, and each time I had to lie my way farther south along Route 5, all to Bill's growing unhappiness. Finally, he asked, "Where in hell do you want to stop, Mother? It's getting kinda late," and I, having adeptly(?) eliminated all the earlier options, quickly suggested that maybe the Wayside Inn, in West Springfield, would be pleasant. It was now nearly 6:20 and this was practically the last place before home. As Bill turned off Route 5, I could see that the Wayside's parking lot appeared to be nearly empty — no company cars were visible, anyhow.

So he pulled in and was gentleman enough to escort me inside. But, as we were a few minutes earlier than I had agreed on with Lou, I suggested we have a drink in the bar before going to the diningroom. As we were sipping our vodka martinis, WWLP's local sales manager, Dan Sullivan,

Engineer Lou Chenevert records FCC-required readings. Early Commission rules required periodic logging of countless television station metrics.

who I knew had helped arrange the event, briefly entered the bar and stammered an embarrassed greeting. So I invented another lie about Danny maybe having to meet some clients. Then, Lou Chenevert, one of our original and favorite engineers, came through with his wife, Rita, and I was forced to invent another lie to explain why an engineer and his wife were somehow involved in a sales meeting. I was fast becoming quite a competitor to Baron Munchausen or Ananias.

By this time, however, my numerous impromptu fabrications had aroused William's suspicions and he gave me a grilling. "What are you up to, Mother? There's something really fishy about both Sullivan and Chenevert being here, too." And so I had to confess my critical part in a conspiracy — to deliver the guest of honor to a surprise birthday party. Then we got up and entered one of the private dining rooms where he could see most of the staff of WWLP, all save the nighttime engineers and talent, gathered to wish him well. Lou Marek had rounded up almost everyone.

I soon learned they had been patiently waiting, with their cars all hidden behind the restaurant, while Bill and I finished our drinks. But that evening event also taught me — a realization that came to me as something of a surprise — that he and I (though not then a legal couple) had created a "Mom and Pop" situation for ourselves at WWLP. It was a very pleasant and rewarding discovery.

Two dozen years later, on October 3, 1981, the Massachusetts Broadcasters Association presented joint awards: To Kitty *"in recognition of your service to the public through television and your dedication to the improvement of the industry locally and nationally."*

And to Bill: *"In recognition of the high standards you have maintained as a broadcaster and your dedication to the belief that service to the public is the foundation of Free Expression."*

Several years after we had left the industry, Bill's son, Lowell, whose computer-based business system for television (VCI) was widely in use across the continent, urged the trade press of broadcasting to recognize his father's major role in building the television industry. So in 2001, Bill was inducted into the Broadcasting Hall of Fame, as the leading figure in

Bill Putnam's 2001 induction into the Broadcasting Hall of Fame; daughters Erica and Karen, mother Kitty at right —"shouldn't have fed those kids vitamins."

the development of the UHF-TV band. Lowell could not attend the induction ceremony in New York, but my two daughters, Karen and Erica, were there to hear Bill's acceptance speech — in which he pointedly upbraided the Selection Committee for not honoring me instead.

◆　◆　◆

I Finally Get a Decent Raise

For many years, in addition to doing the daily show, I continued to serve as Bill's secretary, typing his confidential correspondence, fending off phone callers he did not want to talk with, helping him draft his editorials — so he wouldn't offend everyone in town all the time — and gradually accepting the duty of keeping the other station executives in line when Bill was out of the office and came by with questions.

However, one day I fielded a query from Jim Ferguson, the executive vice-president and general sales manager, who drew down much more than twice my salary, and came to our office demanding to know if it would be possible to preempt the network for a special half-hour program his staff would be able to sell locally. Bill was attending some kind of mountaineering function in California, and Jim couldn't reach him and just assumed I was the boss. So I told him, "I'm not paid to make that kind of decision, Jim; you'll have to do it and take any heat when Bill gets back." Everyone knew that Bill had issued a firm and general order to the effect that WWLP would never preempt NBC, except on his personal order.

Jim left the office and tried again to get Bill on the phone, this time successfully, and apparently was given a brush-off, being referred back to me for a decision. A little while later, Bill called in and gave me hell for not having made the decision in the first place: "You know how to sweet-talk Paul Rittenhouse and those network people, Mother. What's wrong with you?" he ended up asking.

So I told him bluntly, "I deserve a raise if I'm to make decisions like that, straighten out things with the network, and give orders to the executive vice-president."

He temporized, knowing I had a good point, but he needed some cover, calming me down and promising that he'd take care of the matter as soon as he got home.

WWLP's 3rd birthday — Kitty with Roger Putnam.

So, a few days later, Bill finally faced the issue of equal pay for comparable responsibility by drawing up a list of all our station executives — treasurer, program director, chief engineer, promotion manager, news chief — with their rates of pay written adjacent to each name — all except mine — he left a blank where my pay should have been. He asked his father to fill in that blank. Bill's father, a former mayor of Springfield and nationally known business figure, was his closest friend and advisor and would come up to the mountain for lunch almost every week — sometimes he would bring us sandwiches and milkshakes, sometimes I would prepare a luncheon for three in my studio kitchen. I was content with Bill's proposed solution, for I always felt that "Gregor," the family name for Mr. Putnam, was a fair man who would not let outdated prejudices rule. When he filled in that blank number, I got a very substantial raise, as well as elevation to clerk and vice-president of the corporation at the very next board meeting, which was soon followed by a company-supplied car, replacing my, by now, very tired old Ford.

◆   ◆   ◆

Interviews in Washington

It became easier after I was elected to the NAB TV Board, and had another reason to make frequent trips to Washington; but even before then, Bill and I would alternate on lobbying and other trips to the capital, on which we always went up on the 'Hill" to either the Senate or the House studios (depending on who was our principal guest) and taped a half-hour appearance. Mostly, these interviews included "our" Congressmen from the 1st and 2nd Districts of Massachusetts, Republican Silvio Otto Conte, of Pittsfield, and Democrat Edward Patrick Boland, of Springfield. (Two of our children, Erica and Morgan, both started their working careers as summer interns for these members of Congress, Morgan eventually becoming Boland's administrative aide.) They were both fun guests, with Silvio's irrepressible sense of humor and Eddie's inside track on everything going on in the Congress. For each such occasion we would bring along a half-hour of blank videotape from Springfield and take it back home as soon as possible, so the material would not become stale. The politicians preferred me, and often told me so, because I suspect they did not like Bill's frequent insistence on getting simple, definite answers to his questions, for no smart politician likes to give a flat answer to anything.

On one occasion, in the fall of 1973, my guests were Senators Edward Brooke of Massachusetts and Lowell Weicker of Connecticut. A big topic in the news then was the noose slowly tightening about vice-president Spiro Agnew for some of his earlier misdeeds when he was governor of Maryland. Senator Weicker was antsy to wrap up the interview, and he arranged to bow out early because, as he explained, he had a tennis date with Agnew — and he did not want to answer serious questions about a man with whom he had such personal contact. Senator Brooke, on the other hand, had no such ties and was most candid about the vice-president's chances of survival; they were very poor — if he did not go voluntarily, and soon — impeachment was sure to follow.

News cameraman Jim Brady at work.

After ten years, Tom Colton became our primary news anchor, and even did interviews in front of Springfield's City Hall with Mayor William J. Sullivan.

After Weicker left the interview, Brooke told me that the word on the Hill was that Agnew was going to resign the next morning, so I was particularly anxious to get the wrap-up of this interview on our air that very evening. As soon as my plane landed at Bradley Field, I hurried to the mountain with my heavy but precious tape and gave it to our news director, Keith Silver. He grumbled about my insistence that he use excerpts from it that very evening: "Dammit, Kitty, I've just gotten everything timed out for the 6 o'clock period. You can't be serious about my using the whole tape right now."

"Not all of it, Keith, but you go screen the final five minutes and you'll see that we have something here that no other station or network has. Today, Senator Brooke told me that Agnew is resigning tomorrow, and after that happens, this tape will lose a lot of its value."

A Tearful Farewell

Over the nearly twenty years of our acquaintance, I had grown to love Mr. Roger Lowell Putnam, and he treated me as gently and warmly as a daughter. He once told me that he was enormously pleased that Bill had as wise, strong and loyal a female presence as I was to help him run the corporation. When he died of a stroke, just before Thanksgiving Day in 1972, I felt the blow almost as much as did his son, so I told the station staff to pull all the schedule of editorials. Bill had asked me to tape a short bit in explanation that could run a few times during the period prior to Gregor's overflow-attended funeral Mass at St. Michael's Cathedral and burial in the East Road Cemetery of Petersham.

WWLP's second news chief, Keith Silver, presses a question at a local politician.

"I have been asked to speak in this time that is normally allotted to Bill Putnam. This is a personal message from Bill. It was written by him and these are his words.

'I want to thank the many, many people whose expressions of love and understanding have meant so much to my mother and to the children of Roger Putnam. It was most kind of all of you.

'My father was a most privileged person. Few of us are given the pleasure of seeing the many facets of a vigorous life reach maturity and recognition.

'My father died as he lived for 79 years — a forceful example of consideration, integrity and principle. My father died, as he lived for 53 years — in the presence of his devoted and admirable wife.

'He leaves a large hole in the lives of his family, friends and the people of this city, state and nation that he served so long and so well.'"

There was one amusing bit during this otherwise sad event — which was also attended by civic leaders from all over the state, several members of Congress and NBC executives who came up from New York. As the funeral cortege left Springfield's cathedral for the hour-long trip north to Petersham, a State Police cruiser showed up to lead the way. Roger Putnam was noted for his heavy foot while driving — a condition clearly inherited by his son — and was frequently cited for speeding. While following the hearse, Bill observed to those with him in the limousine: "This is the first time the State Police have ever been *in front* of my father going between Springfield and Petersham."

At the graveside, when Gregor's casket had been lowered into the ground, Mrs. Putnam tossed down one red rose, which had been sent by his older sister, Kay, onto the bier and then Bill reached for a nearby shovel to complete the burial, a process in which he was soon joined by his male siblings and relatives. Our Godfather, Joe Deliso, who was also present, was aghast and told them to stop. However, Bill was quick to tell him that "Gregor would have expected this of us. He taught us all that honest labor was not difficult work. Joe! This is the last loving thing we can do for him."

On what would have been his father's 79th birthday, December 19, 1992, Bill referred to him as follows:

> Had he lived, today would have marked the start of my father's 80th year. Since I often plan these statements well in advance, I had already planned to comment on this occasion, some months ago. Though he is gone now, the heritage he has left to his friends, family and the community he served so long and so well, remains even more impressive in his absence. Thus, he merits the same respectful attention he would have received, if here.
>
> Perhaps it is just the pride of a grateful son in a dutiful and honorable father; but I have tried to be detached in my analysis of this matter as in all other subjects. Anyhow, 80 years ago Roger Lowell Putnam was born; and this community was never served more devotedly by any other man in that time. Even though, as his son, I should remember these things, I cannot begin to list the offices he held, or account for the time he gave to city, state and nation, as leader and follower, as guide and prophet, in war and in peace, without ever counting the cost to himself.
>
> A constant example of the right and honorable, a man whose respectful friends would form a line the length and breadth of this state, my father was a real prince. A man whose abilities and interests knew no limits, he could talk geology with me in the mountains and correspond with my brother in Greek. Internationally known in Astronomy, a man whose honors were legion, he always showed the path of true humility and understanding. May we, who his example has touched, be ever mindful of his zest for life, his concept of public interest, his devotion to fair play, and his fond remembrance of friendship.

6

Those Magnificent Irishmen

[KBP] Bill and I wish we could recall all their names, but the effort might include half of the Holyoke Telephone Directory. Their annual parade, scheduled for the Sunday of (or immediately after) St. Patrick's Day, March 17 — a commemoration during which one of us (guess which?) periodically took a perverse delight, as well as his life in his hands, by suggesting to them that the greatest natural disaster in the history of the United States was not the Galveston flood, the Chicago fire or the San Francisco earthquake, but the Irish potato famine. He took further pleasure in reminding them that this date was decreed in 1775 as the state holiday of Evacuation Day, the day and year in which the gun emplacements of Colonel Rufus Putnam (the first Surveyor General of the United States and pioneer settler of Ohio, but unfortunately not an ancestor) on Dorchester Heights had frightened the redcoats into leaving Boston for the less hostile environment of Halifax.

We first thought of televising their St. Patrick's Day Parade down High Street in Holyoke, as soon as we recovered our composure from the Bal de Tête disaster, early in 1955, and approached the management of the citywide festivities. It turned out to be a very acceptable idea on their part, too — the start of a long, cordial and mutually profitable relationship, during the course of which we forged a number of lifelong personal friendships. Obviously none of their wives had been adversely impacted by our earlier remote fiasco.

Over the ensuing years it seemed as if half the world (including, of course, our favorite Irishman, FCC Commissioner Bob Lee) showed up to march in front of our cameras, and almost all of our other station personalities helped me narrate the passing bands, floats and dignitaries. We also learned a lot about positioning the narrators so we could best observe what the cameras were also able to observe.

WWLP's first station manager, local radio veteran Howard Keefe.

The celebration grew greatly over the 28 years we televised it; a Grand Ball soon became part of the event and I had to get all gussied up for the affair which I, being born a Flynn, co-hosted with whichever one of WWLP's station people happened to seem most Irish that year. (We had little trouble with Promotion Manager Howard Keefe; News Chief Edward Martin Kennedy; freelance talent Jack O'Neill; or even Weatherman John Quill; but Rollie Jacobs, while quite adept at the ad-lib, had more difficulty (like Bill) being passed as of sufficiently Irish ancestry. However, my William has told me, many times, that he is descended from Patrick Tracy [1711–1789] "the first horse-thief to be deported from Ireland," who married into the Jacksons when he arrived in Massachusetts, but I'm still unsure of the truth.]

We also televised the annual St. Patrick's Mass, which was generally celebrated by another old and dear friend, Bishop Joseph Maguire. And

A few of those magnificent Irishmen in 1969: Kitty, Jim Malaine, Bill, Maurice Ferriter, Pat Bresnahan.

each day for the two weeks prior to the ball and official coronation, my weekday program included an interview with one of their colleen contestants.

On the Friday afternoon before the parade, Max Marek would drive the remote truck from the mountain to his home on Hitchcock Street in Holyoke, so it would be readily on hand Sunday morning, most often at a position beside the Holyoke City Hall; adjacent to where Bob Vadnais would help fend off prematurely celebrating Irishmen while erecting a special elevated and prefab booth for me and my co-host. Monsieur Vadnais's name was not really Bob, but Hermenus Joseph. He was born in Trois Pistoles, Quebec, and came to us after our request to his uncle, George Vadnais, a major station shareholder, to please find us someone who could build and/or repair everything around a TV station. Bob could, and over the years, did — including all of WRLP on Gun Hill.

One year, when Bill was off skiing in British Columbia with another of our late friends, Hans Gmoser, Ed Kennedy and I were narrating the parade and WWLP had obtained use of a sturdy cherry-picker with basket

WWLP remote setup beside Holyoke City Hall; this feed went across the state.

for one of our cameras, which was positioned high above the center of the street. However, when Ed and I arrived at Bob's stand we were informed there was a tornado alert for the area — a very strong cold front was approaching — but everything started on time, though the wind soon became quite gusty. After the Parade Committee and its president for that year, Maurice Ferriter, had passed our reviewing stand, the wind picked up even more and we could see the bystanders beginning to dissipate, while Bob's special de-mountable box, which housed Ed and me, began to shudder. At this point, Holyoke Police Chief Francis Sullivan stepped up into the booth behind me and said, "OK, Kitty, sign off the parade. That camera has to come down and you two have got to take shelter."

I don't mean to imply that Bill's presence could have prevented any tornado, but since he always brought along an arctic sleeping bag to keep my lower body warm, and he was not there this year, I was happy to oblige the chief before our lonesome cameraman, Al Hedin, as well as our microwave

Top: Cameraman Al Hedin high above the St. Patrick's Day marchers. *Bottom:* Air Force units from Westover Field march past Holyoke City Hall.

Ed Kennedy and Kitty awaiting the tornado in 1956.

dish, got blown away. Fortunately, the area only experienced a strong cold front passage, no tornado. Fortunately also, "shelter" for this grand assemblage of Irishmen and pseudo–Irishmen meant the well-stocked bar of the nearby Yankee Pedlar Inn, and, with the chief at the wheel, his official car soon delivered teetotaling Ed and me right to the door.

My 'Mink' Stole

Speaking of British Columbia reminds me of another friend of Bill's — his collection of mountaineering friends was (and still is) worldwide, and has been unanimously helpful in all of our activities. This time it was the late Ed Wallis, a sometime gold-panner and combination motel/gas station/general store owner beside what Bill described as the "intermittently graveled" Big Bend "Highway" some 80 km upstream from the city of Revelstoke on the Columbia River. This other Ed, whom I never met, apparently also ran a trap line in the steep-sided mountain valley of Downie Creek during the winters. (This whole area is now largely flooded behind the Keenleyside (Revelstoke) Dam, as an outgrowth of the 1961 Columbia River Basin Treaty.)

For years, when I would attend industry and social functions representing the female aspect of our stations, I was always embarrassed by my lack of suitable attire — I mean high-class attire such as a fur coat, etc. So I told William that it was up to him to correct the shortage — on the salary he had long been paying me, I could not afford a fur piece, and those "fisher cat" hides he had gotten me from another friend, Paul Doherty, the ring leader of his "fish cop" buddies in New Hampshire, were just not appropriate. The next summer, he was off again to "the woods," as he put it, meaning the glacier country of southern British Columbia, where he was also the general editor of the climbers' guidebooks. When he eventually returned, in mid–August, he was quick to tell me he had finally solved that "fur piece" issue — I would get a mink stole, and might even be able to wear it by Christmas.

On his way back east, Bill dropped off the stiff hides he had been given by Wallis with Harry Lentfer, a tanner and taxidermist friend of his in Livingston, Montana, and in late October, three silky smooth and lovely furs arrived in the mail. The premier local furrier of Springfield was the late Max Zeller, a Russian émigré who was a longtime fan of Mayor Roger Putnam, an occasional client of the station, and for whom I had frequently modeled furs I could not afford to buy. The next morning, on his way to work, William dropped off the parcel just in from Montana and had a conversation with Max.

But before he arrived at our office up on the mountain, the phone rang. It was Max, and I answered.

"Ver is Meester Putnam, Miss Kitty?"

"He should be here soon, Max," I answered, "I can see his car out in the parking lot, but he always likes to spend some time with the engineers in Master Control before coming up to the office."

"Vell, you tell him, Miss Kitty, dat doze furs he left vith me dis morning may be called mink in de voods of British Columbia, but in my business here, ve call dem zable."

On the Road

One of the "perks" associated with being an on-the-air personality is that travel arrangers often like to build a trip around your name. Bill didn't care for the "mother hen" aspects of such ventures, but it is a part of my nature, so for several years, I took bus tours each autumn to a great variety of interesting places — China, Yugoslavia, Germany, Greece, New Zealand, Norway. For the most part these were uneventful — no hijackings or fatalities — but there was quite a number of interesting episodes, all of which came home to roost on the "trip leader," me. My direct duties consisted mostly of seeing that everyone knew to be "on deck" all packed, breakfast eaten and ready for the day's activities, at an hour which was announced each evening.

However, when one member of an early trip to China got stuck in his bathtub before dinner and couldn't get out, it was me that his wife called, not the hotel front desk. I solved that problem by calling down to the front desk myself. I never learned, and still don't want to know, how that oversized man got extracted from that narrow Chinese bathtub, but he was on time the next morning.

In the Slavic racial mélange that was called Yugoslavia we had a local professional guide for our bus tour, who was very jovial and spoke quite good English. He introduced himself to me, using his long and barely pronounceable Slavic name, but quickly assured me that I could simply call him "Bozo." Several days into the trip it dawned on me how he may have gotten that nickname. I was accustomed to count the bags being loaded onto the bus each morning, to make sure we had everyone's luggage safely with us. On day two, Bozo told me I didn't need to do that chore, I was more useful in other ways, and he was just standing around, so he'd do it for me. But that evening one lady came to me complaining that her bag was missing. I, speaking no Croatian, asked Bozo to see about finding it, which he did quite rapidly, with a phone call to our last hotel. The missing bag was sent along promptly, and the lady got it that very night.

The next day, the genial Bozo did the count again, and that evening two bags were missing, so I accosted him once more, and again he came through with a special delivery. But on day four I stood beside him while he went through the baggage count, and learned — to my considerable dismay — that though Bozo seemed to be very informed about his country and could speak quite passable English, he simply did not know how to count, in any language.

Once, we arrived in Munich at the time of that city's famous Oktoberfest (which is held in September). This is a grand affair and an immense tourist attraction, with every quality hotel filled to capacity, so our party — which included a group from Boston that the airline had attached to my people when the Bostonian "host" failed to enlist a sufficient number of participants on her own — was, perforce, split among more than one hotel. This compounded the difficulty of rounding up people for each day's activities immensely, a situation which I called home to complain about, as the Lufthansa agent for New England had assured me from the start that the whole party was going to be lodged under one roof throughout our tour of Bavaria. Over the next ten days, though we visited a number of scenic and historic places, we only enjoyed that promised condition twice. So, when we finally arrived back at Logan Airport and the regional Lufthansa representative, Bert Klein, greeted me with a big bouquet of red roses I handed them back to him, saying, "You know what you can do with these."

In New Zealand, the tour operator had arranged that every couple would have a farewell dinner in the home of some local family in the Christchurch area. While many of the group were at first reluctant to try

With the Grand Potentates of Melha Temple in 1959. WWLP was using a pair of Marconi studio cameras by then.

such an unusual familiarity, this special and unique act turned out to be a most pleasant and educational experience for all of us.

In Greece, we had a fancy dinner scheduled for our final evening at a hilltop restaurant some distance from our hotel. My party that year included a large shareholder in Springfield Television — Joe Deliso, our godfather, a very practical man but one who was not to be trifled with, and whose wife, Eva, was of Greek origin. Joe and Mrs. Deliso insisted on riding in the same taxi with me to this destination, and when we reached the restaurant and got out of the taxi, Joe told the driver to come back for us at 10 o'clock. According to Eva, the driver grumbled something to the effect that maybe he'd do it — if he didn't get a better offer — whereupon Joe took out a twenty dollar bill and tore it neatly in two, giving the driver one half, and said, "You be back here at ten, and you'll get the other half." After Eva made her husband's proposal perfectly clear, the taxi was early.

In Norway, our travel was by train from Oslo to Bergen, then by ship through the famous fjords as far north as Narvik. My daughter Erica, fresh out of college, came along to be of assistance, as the party was quite large. Once in Norway, we were met by our local guide, a well-spoken law student named Arve Moen, who was sufficiently taken with Erica that they corresponded for several years; even after she was married and Arve had become the principal counsel to StatOil and was often based in such faraway and exotic places as Yemen and Riyadh.

◆   ◆   ◆

Bill's Favorite Guest

Joe Petermann ran an antique shop someplace in Vermont. I was never able to find my own way to this place, but the one time I went there (with someone else doing the driving) I was very impressed with the variety of old and odd things he had amassed in his rickety old barn of a place. It was not organized in a manner that made any sense to me, but Joe knew the exact whereabouts of everything in his "inventory" and could rapidly put his hand on an example of anything that I so much as hinted I would like to see. But Joe's "shop" was not why Bill liked Joe — he never went there, because Joe always came to us.

Bill as a fashion model for Kitty's annual mental health benefit luncheon and remote telecast.

Every few months I would get a call from Joe, who would then arrive on the mountain at the appointed time, complete with his van full of odds and ends. The second time he showed up, he had a big brass bell, which he alleged had come from a Boston and Maine Railroad steam engine. Bill is a railroad buff and was — at that time — a shareholder in Hans Gmoser's Canadian Mountain Holidays, and when he saw that bell, he quickly decided that Hans needed this kind of item for his first and most famous ski lodge in the Bugaboo Range of British Columbia. So Bill made a quick deal with Joe to leave the bell with us on the mountain, and maybe go find another bell or two, as Hans was planning further expansions for CMH.

That summer, Bill delivered the handsome bell to Bugaboo Lodge, where it was soon installed on a special mount outside the front entrance, and he was quick to learn that Hans had firmed up plans for another lodge in the Cariboo Range, which would obviously also require a bell. How he smuggled those bells across the border into Canada was another matter, perhaps by alleging that they had come off a Canadian Pacific engine originally. Anyhow, Bill's donations of bells — acquired through Joe's efforts — soon came to enhance the morning reveille calls at CMH's

Kitty with a special air crew from Westover Field. Note the omnipresent Zoomar Lens #007.

Cariboo Lodge and, more importantly, at the private place which Bill and Hans soon built for themselves — their "abbey" in the Battle Range.

I never got to hear the resounding tenor notes of those bells in the mountains, except for the one at Battle Abbey, which was built with the aid of our children and grandchildren, as well as all the other "volunteers" Bill could round up. But Joe lives in my memory of fun guests and Bill would still like a few more bells — perhaps to resound over Mars Hill, now that the Santa Fe Railroad is no longer required to wake up the town of Flagstaff every ten minutes, day and night, as the multiple engines of their one hundred trains per day formerly blasted the air at the town's five grade crossings.

Beyond Cooking

One of our very best employees was a particularly knowledgeable sports enthusiast named William Rasmussen, who was with us part-time for several years before he approached Bill and me one day with an idea.

Our local news effort needed rejuvenating and a different managerial approach toward coverage. We heard him out and then accepted his ideas, asking him to take overall charge of WWLP's news staff. Soon, under Rasmussen's leadership, our news ratings began to climb even further, and we were very content with the result. However, the man was full of ideas, and clearly needed further fields to conquer. He next suggested I should compose a cookbook, which would also be a station promotional piece. That cookbook became the foundation for the appendix A to this narrative.

So, for several weeks, I spent free moments at home, talking into a tape recorder (while my children giggled at my incipient senility, as demonstrated by my always talking to myself). "Rass" would then have someone reduce the recordings to printed form for further editing. In due course, our press run was several thousand. (Years later, when we migrated to Flagstaff, I added a sequel of new anecdotes and recipes and printed a second edition — some items of which are to be found in appendix B). But Rasmussen was still restless and feeling unfulfilled in his primary interest, so we wished him well as he migrated from WWLP into doing play-by-play for the Hartford Whalers and thence into founding the immensely successful ESPN.

7

Building a Network Relationship

[WLP] As mentioned earlier, when our various initial sponsors woke up to our abysmal lack of audience in the summer of 1953, a fearsome lot of them began to drift away. They wanted results at their cash registers, not ours. So, too, did some of us; Al Tindal had made periodic calls on various network people and had been handling national sales with the same firm that had represented WSPR, the George P. Hollingbery Company. But their agency clients looked at ratings, and we barely made it into the book, despite having a good number of popular network programs. WWLP had purchased the output of Dr. Sydney Roslow–TV Pulse — knowing it to be the most "station-friendly" of the various options; but, unfortunately, very few of the big agencies had much faith in its accuracy.

A year after we had signed on, our initial capital had been used up in buying capital items — cameras, tower, etc. — and our line of credit from the local banks had been maxed out to meet the payroll and keep our doors open. Something had to be done. We drew some comfort from having actually had a cash-flow positive month in March of 1954 and were doing our best to get ever more local people in front of our local cameras. This was a task for *Romper Room* just after the *Today Show*; *At Home with Kitty* later in the daytime, with a great assist from the Western Massachusetts Electric Company's early evening *Highlights* program at 7:15; and our News Department, then under Ed Kennedy's leadership, constantly struggled to get faces and events in front of their film cameras. But we needed more money so we could hold on while we worked to induce people to buy newer TV sets, or external "converters" that could make the old ones receive our signal — and many of us reached down in our pockets.

Kitty took out a second mortgage on her house, I took a 40 percent pay cut — to less than half of the 2010 "poverty level" — and cashed in the last of what Great-aunt Elsie had left for me; most of our existing shareholders and many of our employees put up more money, and my father came through handsomely, as did our "godfather" — Joe Deliso — who really played that part, complete with black homburg hat, a large, isolated estate, just awful cigars, and a big, black Cadillac (everything except a moat with alligators); George Vadnais, the Quebec-born major residence builder of the area; and Anthony Patrick (Bus) McQuade, a saloon-owner, perennial chairman of the Springfield Water Commission and the nearest thing the community had to a political boss. When it came time to put up additional cash, everyone paid by check, all except Bus. He would ask me to drop by his house of an evening and would count out bills, from fives to fifties, always in crinkled condition, but always on time. We later hired his posthumous daughter, Annie, a lovely and talented producer-director. But a number of our other shareholders couldn't, wouldn't, or didn't chip in — much to their ultimate chagrin.

Our second Miss Romper Room, Jan Baker.

Roger Putnam cuts the birthday cake for WWLP's first anniversary while the mayors of Springfield and Chicopee (in 1954) look on; Fred Emerson and "Bus" McQuade on left, banker Bill Lieson on right.

Al Tindal and the co-owner of WSPR, Kris Solberg, were at a loss. Actually, it was their respective wives who inherited the station from their fathers, who had founded it a generation earlier. WSPR had recently shut down its FM station, turning in what was going to be a valuable ticket a few years later — when frequency modulated radio finally came into wide public acceptance — but they had no stomach for a diet of hardtack and beans. They were scared and had no funds to help keep the television station going. Thus we parted company, though staying friendly, and I took over the task of keeping tabs on Hollingbery and staying in touch with the appropriate decision-makers at the networks, all four of them — NBC, ABC, CBS and Dumont (the last of which was soon out of business, but its key stations later became cornerstones of the Fox Network). (Allen Balcom Dumont [1901–1965], a victim of polio in his youth, was a true television pioneer. In addition to making the best origination equipment at the start of television, he put together the first television network, linking his station in New York on Channel 5, WABD, with his collaborator's station in Washington, WTTG. He lacked, however, the strong radio networks of the others as a foundation on which to build a nationwide broadcasting service for the new medium.)

Thus began my routine of visitations to NBC. Every few weeks I would arise before 5:00 A.M. and drive down to New York, arriving there as the Gothamites were getting to work. I would check in at the Hollingbery office, just north of New York's famous public library, and then hike uptown a few blocks to schmooze the networks' affiliate relations people as needed. But it soon became apparent that only NBC was really worth sustained effort on my part, so I spent most of my time getting as close as I could to the hierarchy at 30 Rock. Paul Rittenhouse was NBC's man in charge of affiliations in the Northeast, and he liked me, got us periodic rate increases from the big shots down on the 6th floor, despite our initially dismal ratings, and generally taught me how a good affiliate should behave. I still recall our regular and very pleasant luncheon meetings with various other persons at the English Grille on the north side of the ice rink at 30 Rockefeller Plaza.

In those days, a station's income from network revenue was a minor, but very regular and respected line in every station's P and L statement (the checks came in with perfect regularity on the 20th day of the following month). Many years later, at his retirement in 1977, Paul remarked that he had very much enjoyed our twenty-plus years together and that he and I had thereby again proved the old adage that "There is nothing so permanent as a temporary arrangement." Paul was a tennis buff, and I coerced "his" other stations to chip in for a retirement gift (one-way, first-class airplane tickets for him and his wife, Geri, from New York

A quiet moment of togetherness at a network function; NBC News President Robert Mulholland, behind Kitty.

to Honolulu). However, Paul turned them in for cash and only got as far west as Sedona, near Flagstaff, where we met a few times before his death in 1982.

Subsequently, when our relationship with NBC had become somewhat firmer, I spoke up at what was alleged to be a "closed" meeting of *affiliates only*, suggesting that we should all pressure the network to produce more weekend news and information and "less cartoon-type drivel." Afterwards Paul approached me in the hallway: "Bill, the walls have ears around here; if you want to be of influence with NBC, you should be more careful how you express any criticism. Those Saturday morning kids' shows are very profitable!" Kitty and I got a reiteration of Paul's warning that very evening (though we notice now, in our old age, that my advice has finally been taken seriously).

NBC had the custom of putting on a good farewell show for its affiliates, once a year, and generally in Los Angeles. One year, the USC Trojan Marching Band paraded through the meeting hall, and the late, great Bob Hope was a perennial favorite. At that final evening of this convention all the station operators were to attend a gala dinner at one of the huge Hollywood sound studios, with the legendary, Brooklyn-born Mae West (1893–1980) as guest of honor. Kitty and I found ourselves assigned to a table — behind the potted palms (she said) — near the caterer's trucks, but where we could still see the renowned guest's table, up on a platform. Unfortunately, we were not issued a suitable telescope; though I also well recall one of the bartenders advising me on how to deliver Kitty's request for an after-dinner drink — Grand Marnier — by mixing Cointreau 50/50 with vodka.

◆　◆　◆

Getting Their Attention

It didn't take us long to recognize that there was a very close relationship between broadcasting and politics. Each network hierarchy called for a vice-president in Washington, who was basically their chief lobbyist, and I soon found that prowling the corridors of the Federal Communications Commission was a routine necessity, and that it paid to have influential friends on Capitol Hill. In the aggregate I must have spent several weeks

Greeting the brass of NBC before WWLP's 25th birthday party; David Adams, Julian Goodman, Kitty.

rewriting drafts of my editorials and doing other paperwork while sitting in commissioner or senatorial waiting rooms.

Early in its half-hearted recognition of UHF tribulations, the FCC became convinced that one way to encourage more use of the vast (70 channel) UHF band was to allow broadcasting groups to own up to seven (from the then limit of five) stations, provided the two additional were in the UHF band. So in 1955 NBC acquired WKNB-TV, a station on Channel 30 in Hartford (actually licensed to nearby New Britain), and one in Buffalo; CBS also briefly acquired one in Hartford (on Channel 18) and another in Milwaukee. ABC did nothing and only Storer Broadcasting (among the major non-network owners) took up the opportunity — in Miami and in Boston. However, CBS was soon to dispose of its UHF stations, the one in Hartford being sold to a "pay TV" entrepreneur with the network going to the Travelers' Insurance Company's station on Channel 3.

I saw these purchases as an opportunity to score a useful point and went to an old political friend of my father's, the late John William McCormick, then in the process of assuming the speakership of the House from Sam Rayburn. After a brief talk with John W's brain trust, Eugene Kinnealy, I drafted a letter to the then chairman of NBC, Robert, the son of General David Sarnoff and producer of the famous *Victory at Sea* series. I congratulated NBC on its acquisitions and mentioned as an aside that the McCormicks — John and his younger brother, Edward ("Knocko," who was distinguished primarily for his custom of riding a white horse in the annual St. Patrick's Day parade through much of Boston) — had a long relationship with the Putnams, who also ran an NBC-affiliated television station in Springfield. Gene put this message on the Speaker's letterhead and I waited for a reaction, knowing that, however subtle, the point would not be wasted. (David Sarnoff [1891–1971], a native of Russia, managed to promote himself into the presidency of RCA by 1930, but became a Signal Corps General in 1945 and loved being addressed by that title. He re-established the National Television Standards Committee in 1941 to work up a compatible system for transmitting color. However, the general's alleged part from the rooftop of John Wanamaker's New York store in the *Titanic* rescue of 1912 was largely imaginary.)

Nothing happened! Weeks went by, and still no response to either the new Speaker or myself! I wondered if the letter had ever gone out or had maybe been lost in transit. Then, at the following annual meeting of the affiliates in Los Angeles, as Kitty and I were passing through the receiving line, Don Mercer, manager of affiliate relations, introduced me to David Adams, the network's executive vice-president and *eminence grise*, who turned to introduce me to Robert Sarnoff, saying: "Bob, this is Bill Putnam, who owns our Springfield affiliate, and who is such a good friend of Speaker McCormick." I knew immediately that though nothing had appeared to happen, a great deal had indeed occurred.

Dinner at Le Pavilion

Two years later, NBC decided to dispose of that station on Channel 30, and we made a bid for it, in conjunction with Herbert ("Buzzie")

Scheftel, Albert Burger and Elmer Balaban. In dickering over price with NBC's "Buddy" Sugg, then vice-president in charge of NBC's owned and operated stations, we were shown its operating statements and I asked, "If it's such a great property and you're making 20 percent net profit, how come you want to sell it?"

"I simply don't want to own a station that doesn't return 40 percent on its gross."

Though Springfield Television did not close as part of that sale, because of the FCC's then "overlapping ownership" restrictions, we stayed friendly with Buzzie (whose parents were among the missing passengers on the *Titanic*) and his associates. One afternoon, as we were wrapping up a discussion in the 56th Street office of Al and Buzzie's Trans-Continental Properties, he suggested we all adjourn for dinner. "Where would you like to go, Bill?"

"Hell, I dunno, Buzzie. Anything you select is OK. I'm just a country boy, anyhow."

Buzzie then turned to Elmer Balaban, who had come in from Chicago, "Any place you'd like to go, Elmer?"

"No, Buzzie; I'm like Bill. You and Al are natives here. Pick a spot you like."

At this point Al Burger spoke up. "Oh! Buzzie, let's go to Le Pavilion, after all, we own that."

In the conversation on the three-block hike over to Le Pavilion, we found out that these sophisticated property investors did not own the super-chic restaurant after all; instead they owned the multi-story, block-wide, mid–town Manhattan building in which it was located.

On another visit to the Transcontinental Properties office, I was talking with Al Burger when his phone rang. I got up to go out of his office but Al motioned me to remain, so I heard his side of a lengthy conversation that pertained to the famous Mark Hopkins Hotel in San Francisco. After he had hung up, Al explained that he had just concluded the final stage of a three-part deal he had been working on for some time. He and Buzzie now owned [1] the land on which the building was located, [2] the building itself, and [3] the business of running a hotel in that building. Now that they had it all reassembled, I asked if they might be willing to celebrate by doing me a small favor.

"Of course," said Al, "what's on your mind?"

I explained that I had a good friend who was chief of the Northern

Division of New Hampshire's Fish and Game Department. Paul Doherty's wife, Barbara, was dying of cancer and had always wanted to visit Hawaii. But on his game warden's salary, Paul could not afford to pay for a decent hotel in San Francisco on their way to and from Hawaii. Was there some way he could help out?

"There surely is, Bill," replied Al, handing me a business card. "Just give him this, and have him call me when he has his travel schedule firmed up."

Thus it was that Mr. and Mrs. Paul Thomas Doherty, of Gorham Hill, New Hampshire, stayed in the Presidential suite at "the Mark," both coming and going to Hawaii, with dinner and wine on the house.

(My closeness with the "fish cops" of New Hampshire, which dated from being their resource when called upon, as required by state law, to provide for the rescue of people lost in the woods, resulted in my being regularly invited to attend their mid–winter "game dinners"— at which the game wardens and their wives would offer a variety of exotic recipes, the formulae for which I always brought back for Kitty's education. But, no matter how strongly I urged her, she never could bring herself to offer tips on the air for preparation of North Country delicacies such as jellied moose nose, wild onion soup, mountain cranberry sauce, or sautéed bracken fiddle heads.)

◆   ◆   ◆

The Affiliates' Board

Some time later, one evening at a multi-day Television Affiliates' Board meeting with the network brass on Maui, when I was one of the senior affiliate representatives and the group's secretary/treasurer, I was seated at one of those little, dinky round tables they have in cocktail lounges, talking with another board member. During the formal sessions earlier in the day, David Adams and I had been the lead spokesmen in exchanging somewhat opposing views on an issue and we had agreed to constitute ourselves as an *ad hoc* "committee of two," to continue the discussion over a drink, so as to help arrive more quickly at a formal agreement the next morning. Adams walked into the carpeted cocktail lounge, came over to where I was and put his drink on the table to kneel down on one knee and chat. At this point, my companion stood up and said:

"Hold everything! I know you guys have an issue to settle, but first I gotta get a picture of this: David Adams down on his knees to a UHF operator."

The Affiliates' Board was made up of eight affiliated station operators who served overlapping four-year terms — actual owners were preferred because they could speak with greater authority and effectiveness, and the chairman was generally someone from a major market, and/or who had other status in the broadcasting industry, such as Jack Harris from Houston, Hod Grams from St. Louis, or Ancil Payne from Seattle — the idea being that when such an affiliate executive delivered a message on behalf of the more than 200 other stations, it would be heard more clearly by the brass on the 6th floor. Unfortunately, my years as a member of the NBC Affiliates' Board coincided mostly with the reign of Fred Silverman, when the peacock network's fortunes sank to an all-time low, and the Affiliates' Board was largely occupied with holding the network together.

One of the most tedious chores that befell me during those years was that of reasoning with Jane Cahill Pfeiffer, a onetime postulant nun, who had been named by the executives of RCA as CEO of NBC in 1978 (to help Freddie Silverman, who was an experienced program-producing executive but seemed to know little about the business of broadcasting). Jane was a nice lady, experienced in corporate public relations at IBM, but she was also woefully ignorant of our business, as was obvious to the Affiliates' acting chairman Blake Byrne and me after she made life so difficult for David Adams and Julian Goodman, both of whom really knew the broadcasting business, that they opted to retire. I recall walking up and down (actually east and west) along the south corridor of NBC's 6th floor executive offices for more than one extended, private, and intense but ultimately unproductive conversation with her about the realities of broadcasting. (Finally, and with a great sigh of relief from all the affiliates, the people at RCA got smart, parting with both Freddie and Jane, and engaged the services of Grant Tinker, a man whom we could all trust and admire, to run the NBC show.)

In even later years, when NBC wanted an audience with Speaker Thomas Patrick "Tip" O'Neill, their Washington VP, Peter Kenney, whom we had known earlier when he was the manager of WKNB-TV, struck out with getting its Boston affiliate to do the job and asked if Kitty and I would arrange for and accompany them to such a meeting. Since Kitty's son, Morgan, was then Eddie Boland's chief of staff, this was not at all difficult for us to set up; our Eddie Boland was in the same congressional "class" as Tip and the two had shared a Washington apartment for many years. When we all arrived at the Speaker's office at the appointed hour, it turned out that the great man was closeted with others, but as soon as his receptionist sent in word that we were waiting, he burst out of his inner sanctum and grasped Kitty in an enormous bear-hug; then he turned to me and asked gently how my mother was bearing up in her widowhood. Finally, he looked over at them and said to the NBC brass, who stood around, gaping, "Gentlemen, what can I do for you? You've come here in very good company." (PS: In 2010, with both of us long out of any active role in the industry, and in finishing up this narrative, we reminisced at some length with Pete in the living room of his retirement home in Henlopen Acres, on Delaware Bay.)

Wrestling on Cue

Before we clinched our full-time relationship with NBC, WWLP carried occasional programs from the other networks, which included the *Wednesday Night Wrestling from Chicago* at 9:00 on ABC-TV. My mother, an otherwise virulent prude, enjoyed this program, much to Kitty's amazement, and would subsequently regale me with narrations of events in this tumbling match program that I found to be more laughable than much that was passed off as comedy.

What my mother may not have appreciated was that this program came to the stations on a "co-operative" basis — that is, the stations carrying *Wrestling* were given an opportunity to sell commercials within the body of the hour-long program, which was formatted by ABC for such local insertions. Unfortunately, we were also required to account to ABC and share any such revenue. Our salespeople apparently were able to find sufficient folk like my mother to make a few such sales, and every Wednesday afternoon, ABC would send down a teletyped format of the evening's program, so the stations would know when and where they could insert their local commercials. Interestingly, this TWX message also told us who was going to "win" each such bout of these "contests," and when — but not how.

On the occasion of her 90th birthday, November 16, 1982, Caroline Putnam (1892–1993) appeared as a guest on Kitty's show and discussed her long and eventful life, from her childhood as the elder daughter of a country farmer and sometime doctor, living near Pomonkey in Charles County, Maryland, to the present. (The lady never graduated from high school, having been called home to help care for her ailing father and six younger brothers, but in later years she received more than a dozen honorary doctorates for her work in helping the African-American minority in America to receive advanced education. She met her husband late in 1917 when he was a naval lieutenant plotting the range characteristics for the 14-inch guns of the newly commissioned battleship *Mississippi*, and she was the volunteer base librarian at the naval gunpowder factory at nearby Indian Head, of which her brother, Thomas, was later to be superintendent.)

I brought her up to the studio at the appointed hour and the two of us took her back home afterwards. However, this erudite guest may have embarrassed hostess Kitty, when, toward the close of the program, she was asked about the process of growing old, and talked on through the time of Kitty's normal sign-off patter (the production crew and engineers would not have dared to cut my mother's mike), ending with a verse from Robert Browning's 1864 poem "Rabbi Ben Ezra":

> Grow old along with me; the best is yet to be,
> The last of life, for which the first was made.
> Our times are in His hand, who said, 'A whole I planned;'
> Youth shows but part. Trust God! Nor be afraid.

◆　◆　◆

Wide, Wide World

For several years, NBC-TV had a program with this title. It was a 90-minute, Sunday afternoon offering, appearing every six to eight weeks. For this show, a single theme was carried throughout, often by a consistent host-narrator, but with pickups from all around the country. In the days before every remote pickup was bounced off some satellite, each such program had to be accomplished using a series of often specially built AT&T microwave links, which would take all the various originating feeds to the network switching headquarters in New York before being sent around the country to the affiliated stations. It was an expensive and enormously complicated show, with cues and timings prearranged down to the second.

At WWLP, we loved to do originations for this program — our price was right, our engineers were union (NABET — Local 13), but quite tolerant on "jurisdictional" issues, while everyone in the station enjoyed earning a lot of overtime, starting on the prior Tuesday, and a great many of us got to go to several interesting localities. Most of our older employees had also become shareholders in Springfield Television — they were welcome to study our annual operating statement and balance sheet — a condition that greatly enabled them to appreciate our informal and paternalistic style of management. In toto, we did *Wide, Wide World* and other network originations, from a rollicking Polish wedding in nearby Westfield, to the somberness of Franklin Roosevelt's home at Hyde Park, NY, as well as several *Today* and *Tonight* pickups from interesting places such as the March of Dimes memorial from the top of Mount Mansfield, Vermont.

Hyde Park was where I saw my first and only four-channel television set, with its cathode-ray projection tube mounted vertically and aimed at a large, slanted mirror, a gift to the president from General Sarnoff. The late newscaster Frank Blair (1930–2009), a *Today* show regular, became our station's favorite talent guest for WWLP anniversary events.

That Polish wedding was held in Westfield's Stanley Park — named in honor of the city's foremost citizen, the late Stanley Beveredge, founder of Stanley Home Products — and within sight of almost every inch of WWLP's tower. For the benefit of those non–Slavs who may never have attended such an affair, it is customary for many of the guests, particularly the males, to help fund the party, as well as provide a wedding gift by stuffing folding money into the bride's bodice. However, NBC's chief censor, Herminio Traviesas, was in the routine custom of perpetually advising all and sundry that the network's inflexible policy was "*No frontal, backal or sideal nudity*" — so we had to be especially careful what our cameras were pointed at, in this case a particularly inviting and prominent vista.

◆ ◆ ◆

Sugaring Off

In mid–March of 1960, we were scheduled to do a pickup from a location near Rutland in west-central Vermont, where the main talent would be America's beloved Yankee poet, Robert Frost. Our first crew was already on the scene, locating camera positions and stringing cables around a rambling old farm, which had been turned into a country inn. But, just before noon on the preceding Wednesday morning, I got a telephone call from the NBC producer in New York.

"We're gonna hafta cancel the program for Sunday."

"Huh? You can't do this to me — I've got one crew already up there, and another leaving within the hour."

"Sorry about that. But Frost says he won't do it."

"How come? I've met him a couple of times, and he's always seemed reasonable and a lot of fun."

"Well, he isn't so damn reasonable, now. We've got the whole show hung on his narration and now he says he just can't do what we want. So, we're gonna hafta scrub the whole thing."

"Wait a minute! If you can hold off that decision for 24 hours, I'll charge up there right now, and try talking to him."

"OK, if you insist. But I'm not optimistic. You'll call me before this time tomorrow?"

So, armed only with the producer's phone extension number at NBC, I promptly left the station to Kitty and what was left of our staff— another bunch of the troops would be riding with me — and headed north for Vermont.

Several hours later, when I arrived at the quaint old inn near Rutland, I went to look up the great poet's secretary to see if I could ferret out the truth about this decidedly uncharacteristic behavior.

"He doesn't like that script!" the lady informed me.

Gently, I told her that the network people knew he had signed a contract for the job, and it was enforceable in court. Backing out now could be damaging. At this news, she flickered, but carried on bravely.

"You know, young man," she went on, "it is a bit presumptuous for some young whippersnappers in New York City to be picking out words for Mr. Frost."

I had to agree, so I tried another tack, my fall-back position. "Tell me, Miss, has he ever mentioned Amy Lowell to you?"

"Oh! Many times! She was his patroness, got him introduced to literary agents and publishers. But that was many years ago, and Miss Lowell is dead, you know."

"Yes, I know; Amy Lowell was my great-aunt."

"You come with me, young man! Mr. Frost is just down the hall in the drawing room."

Within a few seconds, the secretary explained my relationship to

Amy Lowell to her employer at which I could see a twinkle in the old man's eye and felt a glimmer of hope in my plan. So I set out to explain some of the realities of live television programming to the great poet. All across the nation technicians would be looking at copies of the same script he had, which told them when to switch audio (and/or video) from one origination point to another, using the times and words established on the script he was to deliver. They were all especially intent on his final few words in each of the several segments that we were to be originating.

As one who understood — far beyond most of humanity — the effective use of timing in delivery of words, Frost readily grasped this key element in the whole show. "But you know, young man, we're dealing with sugaring-off season here in Vermont and nobody around these parts would talk like that." He pointed to the pile of papers he had tossed onto the floor.

Having already seen part of the script, I had to confess that he had a point. "If you would you excuse me a minute, sir? I think I can solve this impasse, but I'd like to make a phone call."

I was soon in touch with the producer in New York. "Hey! I've been talking with Frost. He's a most reasonable man, but your people have put words into his mouth that are just plain unsuitable for him."

"Yeah! So what? He's got a contract, and he won't live up to it."

"Listen to me a minute!" I felt like really bawling him out for such a crass attitude, but bit my tongue in the hope of salvaging something, for by now WWLP was on the hook for a lot of overtime and other costs that, if the program was scrubbed, NBC might not want to pay for. "You and I both know that all you really care about is his last sentence, as long as he sticks to the subject and takes the right amount of time."

There was a long, l-o-n-g pause, while the producer pondered. "You actually think you can work that out?"

"Trust me! We're on very good terms right now. I'll call you back when I'm sure I've saved your program. OK?"

"Yeah, I guess so." A scrub at this point would have been equally embarrassing to the producer, for the upcoming program had already received a lot of promotion. "OK!"

So I went back to the drawing room and America's iconic Yankee poet, where I found the pile of papers still on the floor. "Mr. Frost, I think we can dispense with that pile but you and I should go over the whole show. I've arranged with the producer that you can do your part of it your way."

Thus it was that the following Sunday afternoon, I dressed Robert Lee Frost (1874–1963) in a Lavelier microphone with a short "tail" that hung out of his bearskin coat. We walked together in the late winter's mud and slush around the old farm, from the gaunt maple trees with their attached buckets, to the stables whence the big, Percheron farm horses pulled sleighs with their huge wooden barrels, to the sugaring-off building, with its large, steaming tray of boiling sap. At each stop, we would look at the program monitor and I would connect his "tail" to a pre-positioned mike cord and cue him when to start his "patter." The venerable Yankee would intone a few appropriate lines about whatever was going on in front of cameras all across the country, both ours and those from the other originating stations, and then I would give him the standard two-minute, one-minute, and thirty-second cues, and finally hold up a big white card with those critical last few words that all those technicians, all across the country (especially that producer, back in New York) were waiting to hear, and into which the great poet would gracefully segue without hesitation.

He loved it, and the show was a great success.

Skiing at Stowe

Our friendship with Frank Blair came about when we were asked to do the origination for *Today* from Mount Mansfield, in Vermont, on the top of which a massive granite "dime" has recently been placed to commemorate the 40th anniversary of President Roosevelt's March of Dimes effort to eradicate the often crippling disease of poliomyelitis, from which he — most famously — suffered.

We had all our Dumont cameras on hand, the regular two from the remote truck and two taken from WRLP for the occasion, but one of them had to be at the top of Mount Mansfield for the unveiling of the granite dime. Fortunately, the transmitter site of WCAX-TV ("Red" Martin's station) was at the summit, so our engineer on duty didn't have to stand out in the January cold, but the CBS affiliate did not have at that location any of the spare items or tubes often needed for replacement when a Dumont camera was reassembled in a new location after being disassembled elsewhere. Thus it came about that we needed a messenger to respond to several crisis calls during our set-up process, the day before the actual origination.

Having the *Today* show originate on the premises of the Mount Mansfield Corporation in Stowe was a good promotional gimmick for New England's most famous ski area, and I had been given a free pass to perform the duties of such a messenger. This enabled me to try out all of the various trails that went from the very top of "Stowe" to the base station and, that early in the season, none of them were very good. One evening, I learned something about ski condition reporting when I approached Sepp Rusch, the Austrian-born general manager, and commented, "I see that you are posting the ski conditions here as 'Good to Excellent' but I have found that the rocks and stumps are sticking up through the ice on all your summit trails. How come 'Excellent'?"

"Vell, it is all r-r-relative [he rolled his R's so charmingly]. On dis mountain, ve haf de only schnow in all of New England, und zo — by compar-r-r-ison to ever-r-ry other-r-r place — it is eggsellent."

The major talent for the *Today* program was missing at Stowe — the irascible J. Fred Muggs having long since been retired (along with Dave Garroway); Hugh Downs was on vacation near Phoenix and Jack Lescoulie's agent said his contract did not require him to go to "such a dangerous and unusual location." So Frank Blair was what we got, and he came through magnificently — though we did notice that there was a glass of some light brownish liquid under his chair, from which he took an occasional generous sip when not on camera and which kept being refilled by one of the network's grunts, between his interviews with the March of Dimes people.

◆   ◆   ◆

Good Night, Chet

At NBC, when roaming about the huge premises of 30 Rock, I once found the opportunity to seek out the office (overlooking the Avenue of the Americas) of the network's resident scholar and intellectual, Edwin Harold Newman (1919–2010), who was a few years older than me, and persuade him to come visit Springfield for a guest appearance as part of the community's adult education program, which was then headed by

Kitty. On another occasion I was able to initiate a respectful friendship with that man's man and our network's prize-winning newscaster, Montana-born Chester Robert Huntley (1911–1974), with whom I was able to share reminiscences of a lengthy childhood summer spent in his home state. Chet unfortunately managed to smoke himself into an early death, some time after delivering himself of a prize line about his co-anchor, the highly touted (having received several Peabody Awards and Emmies) and late David McClure Brinkley, whom Chet referred to once as being among "the actors and jugglers" and who was not on camera with him during one evening newscast because of an American Federation of Radio and Television Actors (AFTRA) strike against NBC. In our old age, we are proud that we still own autographed copies of Ed's and Chet's biographical writings — *Strictly Speaking* and *The Big Sky.*

Butte, Montana, was the home base of a distinguished broadcaster, Edmund Blodgette Craney (1905–1991), with whom we, as smaller community broadcasters, had much in common. Ed's "XL" and "Skyline" networks in western Montana and adjacent Washington suffered greatly from the importation — via cable systems — of their own (mostly NBC) network programs from Salt Lake City and other major markets. I used to plan time on my annual trips to British Columbia to visit with Ed at his home among the cottonwood trees around his AM radio transmitter, at Rocker, just west of Butte. Ed was a great proponent of building low-power translators to enhance the service areas of stations in less densely populated areas, and WWLP had two such devices to further the WRLP signal — channels 79 in Claremont, New Hampshire, and 81 in White River Junction, Vermont.

However, the boys (my son, Lowell, and Kitty's son, Morgan) who invariably accompanied me to the mountains found that Ed's carefully adjusted slot machine (to simply break even) was a far greater attraction than sitting in on my politicking with Ed. Someone had advised Ed, at an early age, to cultivate his nearest United States senator, so he had even dedicated a room in his home for exclusive occupancy by the Massachusetts-born maverick senator from Montana, Burton Kendall Wheeler (1882–1975). Since Wheeler was defeated in a primary election in 1946 and soon went on to wherever such figures go, Ed allowed me to occupy the "Wheeler Room" during my annual overnight visits.

◆　◆　◆

Wide, Wide World—A Woman's View

[KBP] It was one thing to go off on one of those adventures, but quite another to see that nothing goes wrong at home, while half the staff is off gallivanting with big shots. On another such occasion, Bill and the boys scrounged the two cameras they could borrow from the late WWOR as well as all we could spare at home, a grand total of six, and went off to the Saint Lawrence Seaway project, then under serious construction. They were going to originate their part at the Eisenhower Locks, just upstream from Montreal.

I, the unappreciated mother hen, was supposed to keep everything running back on the mountain at WWLP. But, many months earlier, Bill had invited the members of Springfield's Exchange Club to hold a clambake on that particular Friday evening at the station, on the front lawn. I didn't mind being hostess for a number of sponsors, and occasionally even being in charge of the whole station, by now I accepted those as part of my job, but this gang was strictly his, there were few of the station's

Kitty received the Abe Lincoln Award from the leader of the Southern Baptist Convention; Sol Taischoff, publisher of *Broadcasting*, on right.

Mae Mulroney, of New England Liquor Suppliers, presents Kitty with champagne for WWLP's 17th anniversary.

clients among them — none of mine — and he was in farthest upstate New York when the rains came.

The clambake was forced indoors — to my corner of the studio and its kitchen, but only after some of the Exchangites had dug a big hole in the station's front yard, which was now rapidly filling with water. Soon, with another crack of thunder, the entire Exchange Club was inside. Meantime, the beer was flowing, and the *Early News* was about to go on, followed by the station's premier local program, *Western Massachusetts Highlites*. It took some doing to hush everyone and shoo them off to elsewhere in the building, but a good many just wanted to hang around and see a live program from inside the studio.

That Friday evening was awful! Everything got wet and mud was tracked into my living room set, where a dozen men sat around, but (I'll admit) were silent as mice during the broadcasts; though I later found several empty beer cans that had been left behind the furniture. When

The studious person who came up with the correct number of "22s" on this VW bug (which was displayed at shopping malls all over western New England) won a seven-day, all-expense-paid trip for two to the Caribbean on WWLP's 22nd birthday.

everyone was back at work on Monday, I told William he had to fix that hole in the lawn, all by himself, and be quick about it because I had an outdoor gardening show arranged for the next day.

At the end of our first eight years on the mountain, the Arthur C. Nielsen Company credited WWLP with reaching 431,440 homes in the Connecticut Valley, a fact we were proud to crow about. The staff of WWLP now numbered more than eighty. *Printers Ink* had called Bill Putnam "versatile and candid" while *Fortune* had praised his "youthful leadership." I had received two national awards from *McCall's* magazine, and an Abe Lincoln Award for my work in airing the plight of the epileptics and other unfortunates housed in the Massachusetts State Hospitals at Monson and Belchertown. We had worked hard, done our best, and now hoped we were on a roll while we looked for new worlds to conquer.

8

Building Advertiser Support

[WLP] One day during a National Association of Broadcasters (NAB) Convention being held in Chicago, mostly in the Conrad Hilton Hotel, and at which all the sales representative firms maintained "hospitality" suites for their clients, I spotted the big boss, the late George Phillips Hollingbery, glad-handing some other station operators. After waiting for a free moment, I asked him if he knew of a suitable place where I could take Kitty to dinner that evening, as she was due to return home early on the morrow in time to do her show the following afternoon. "I'd like it to be up high, George, if you can find such a place, where she can enjoy the view."

Without batting an eye, he responded, "I'll arrange for the Tavern Club, Bill. That's on the top floor of the building just north of my office. Is 6:30 this evening OK? You know where that is, right?"

Thus, she and I enjoyed a fine dinner, starting with vodka martinis and including a nice bottle of Chardonnay, all while witnessing a magnificent display of lightning theatrics out over Lake Michigan. The lady was very impressed and before leaving the airport in the morning, she called George to thank him.

When I got back to the mountain two days later, the bill from the Tavern Club was already on my desk. George couldn't afford to live in that big house in suburban Glencoe by being unduly generous to people like us.

Without Kitty to control my baser instincts, the following evening I went exploring in the adjacent Blackstone Hotel. Taking the elevator to the 11th floor, I followed the noise to a big corner suite, where I witnessed a massive poker game in progress. There were about a dozen players at this big, round table, with huge amounts of cash visible (enough to buy a major interest in most UHF stations), and a circle of kibitzers behind

123

them. I spotted Phil Dean, who did occasional public relations work for us, among the bystanders and as I eased my way around the table to his side, I heard someone cry, "Hey, Governor, it's your turn. Bet!"

A few hands later, the same person was talking with the advisers behind him and was again dilatory at betting, and one of the others burst out, "Hey, Ambassador, it's your turn again. Bet!"

A third time this player was not paying close attention to the game, and one of the others spoke up loudly, "Hey, you old son-of-a-bitch, you're holding up the game again. BET!"

"Who is that guy?" I whispered to Phil.

"Oh! The guy who's so slow on the betting, that's Horace Hildreth, and they were right each time. He's a lawyer, a former governor of Maine, a former ambassador to Pakistan. He owns the CBS radio station in Portland and is a long-time Republican Party loyalist."

◆   ◆   ◆

Dear Old Evvie

I made many sales calls with Hollingbery's Chicago people. Two such visits I recall in particular. One was to an aging but enormously important buyer named Evelyn Vanderploeg, at Wrigley's in-house agency, just up the street and across the Chicago River from Hollingbery's office. Every sales manager and station operator in the country was polite to Evvie, for she had firm control over an enormous budget and was in the custom of bypassing any intermediaries she didn't approve of, and dealing directly with station principals. Apparently she liked me, because she was quick to accept the pitch I laid on her for Wrigley's entire budget for western Massachusetts.

Some time later, at another NAB convention in Chicago, I was in a meeting room with Jack Harris and some of the other TASO (about which, more below) directors when Evvie poked her head through the door. All the others ignored her, for Evvie was no beauty queen, and most of these guys had only heard of her but never actually encountered this key element in their station's prosperity. I decided to repay the bet she had placed on me.

"Evvie," I spoke up, "Come on in and let me introduce you to some of my friends."

When I learned that she had died in that air crash near Tell City, Indiana, a few months later, I said a short but fervent prayer. Evvie Vanderploeg was a great lady and a good friend.

On another occasion in Chicago in 1958, the agency buyer for Pall Mall cigarettes inquired about setting a start date for a buy she had just made on WWLP. "How soon can you get this schedule started, young man?"

"How soon can you get the filmed commercials to the station? We can get you on the air immediately. Want me to take 'em home this afternoon?"

The lady picked up her intercom phone and spoke to someone on another floor. "I'll have the films sent up right away."

So we sent a TWX to start the Pall Mall schedule that very evening; I'd have the commercials with me.

But when I presented myself at O'Hare Airport early that afternoon, I heard the PA system blare out: "*United Passenger Putnam, William Putnam, please pick up a white courtesy telephone.*"

I soon learned that Kitty had been trying all over Chicago to reach me and that she had an urgent message from Paul Doherty in New Hampshire; I was needed for a rescue high on the spectacular granite cliff of Cannon Mountain. I should call him right away for details.

I did as directed and learned that it was now body-removal only. Then I called Kitty back: "See if you can line up Rob Wallace to go up-country with me; I've told Doherty to save us a room at the Perkins Motel in Littleton. Tell Ed Kennedy to arrange for road courtesy with the state police. We'll get up there as soon as we can after I land at Bradley Field, but I'll have some commercials for you to take back to the mountain for the Pall Mall sked that starts tonight."

The drill on these rescue events was for the "fish cops" to arrange and perform the prosaic but very tedious grunt work of off-trail stretcher service, while I handled the technical aspects of things up on New Hampshire's cliffs. Rob Wallace was a protégé of mine in mountaineering that I had brought along on numerous trips, and I knew him to be strong and reliable. While Kitty saw to the Pall Mall commercials, Rob and I made it to Littleton by 9 P.M., when we learned other details. The fatality was

high on a route called "Sam's Swan Song," pioneered some years earlier
on the tallest part of the Cannon cliff by Theodore P. (Sam) Streibert, and
it involved David Koop, a son of the highly respected surgeon general,
C. Everett Koop.

Early the next day, accompanied by David Isles, who had been party
to the first ascent of Sam's route, Rob and I clambered up the extensive
talus pile below New England's most prominent cliff, on the easterly edge
of which was then to be found the famous profile that had become the
Granite State's emblem. (Unfortunately, an abnormally heavy rainstorm
in early May of 2003 so lubricated the mountaintop and all the turn-
buckles and other restraining paraphernalia which had been installed to
preserve it, that most of New Hampshire's great stone face, which had
been immortalized by Daniel Webster and Nathaniel Hawthorn, as far
back as 1850, came loose and crashed down to join the talus below.) Then
the three of us climbed swiftly to the penultimate pitch, some thousand
feet up the cliff—carrying several long climbing ropes. Doherty and his
gang of game wardens (the stretcher detail) came up more slowly and
stayed at the bottom of the actual cliff.

Dave knew some details of the accident. It seemed that in preparation
for the final pitch, young Koop had driven a piton under a large boulder
to provide a secure anchor. Unfortunately the boulder turned out to be
not very firmly attached to the mountain, and it took the occasion of this
relatively minor disturbance to slide out of place, taking the Dartmouth
junior with it and crushing his lower leg in the process. His partner's
belay had held, but Koop fell nearly 150 feet with his lower leg still barely
attached and bled to death within minutes. I had seen the long streak of
his blood for 500 feet down the cliff, and had even found a piece of the
lad's shinbone while preparing for the ascent.

While I handled the belays for the other two, Rob and Dave soon
lowered the body to Doherty's stretcher gang on the ground and our part
in the day's work was done. By way of a sequel, I received a long and very
gracious hand-written letter of thanks from the surgeon general — the
only such message I ever received from a score of such efforts.

One of my earlier "rescues" had also been on this same cliff, but some
hundreds of feet to the east, on a route known as the "Old Line" because
it was the first to be done on this cliff, in the 1920s. It was also another
'body removal' but one in which I played to the traditional "cast of thousands," for that ghoulish mid–summer hypothermic fatality (which

involved two under-prepared teenagers) had been slow in the making but in the news prominently and vacationers from all over the White Mountains lined the highway below, including Governor J. Wesley Powell, whom Doherty facetiously asked to arrange a charge account for me at the state's various courthouses, because of his frequent need for my high-angle climbing services.

❖ ❖ ❖

A Friend in the Business

Some years later, after George Hollingbery had gone to where all good sales reps go, and Harry Wise was heading the successor company, now called H-R, I got a call from George Hemmerle, the straw-boss manager of their San Francisco office, with whom both Kitty and I had developed strong personal friendships.

"Just calling you, Bill, to say 'goodbye.'"

"Goodbye! Are you quitting, George?"

"Hell, No! I've just been fired."

"FIRED! What's going on?"

"Harry said that since our business from the West Coast has been dropping, they've determined that I'm the problem."

I had not noticed any falling off at our stations, all three of which were represented by the same firm, so I looked more deeply into the matter and found that any decline seemed mostly from the Los Angeles office, which was still managed by Hollingbery's son-in-law, Roy Edwards. I dialed up the New York office, where Harry Wise presided.

"Harry! I just wanted to tell you that I've been thinking we might be smart to change 'rep' firms."

"What's wrong, Bill? I thought we've been doing very well for you."

"I gather that there's a problem on the West Coast; and you've just fired our best producer, Hemmerle; so I figured that if you can fire the guy we feel happiest about, we can fire you. It's that simple."

(Hans Georg Hemmerle, whose father had jumped ship from a Nord-Deutscher Lloyd liner visiting New York in the mid–1920s, and short-order cooked his way across the country to end up as head chef at Yosemite Valley's famous Ahwanee Hotel, stayed on with H-R until after we sold

Provin Mountain from the air; the Springfield Water Department's tanks are at the upper right, one mile north of WWLP. The world's first "live" rock-climbing program originated on the cliffs at lower left, starring our leader.

our stations, when he, too, retired; but we still meet occasionally in the Bay Area and in the mountains.)

A Mountaineering First

Provin Mountain was not the place for that great event for alpinists, a "first ascent," but it did earn a small place in the log books of televised climbing (wherever such things might be kept). In late May of 1956, I talked with Tom Colton about doing a live rock climb on *Western Massachusetts Hilites*. He was amenable and so we used our "remote cameras," as we did for Kitty's swimming pool events, but out to the southwest of the station, rather than northwest, to an area where the cliff on the west side of the mountain was semi-respectable. Unfortunately for me, the cliff required a lot of "cleaning" before one could trust the durability of its handholds, etc. So I had to spend several hours the prior weekend preparing it for the live event on television.

That having been done with an acceptable degree of assurance, the actual climb was a bit of a sham, as I had also put several fixed (tied to the trees above) ropes in place so we could demonstrate the art of rappelling, as well as the process of climbing on such tenuous terrain as this crumbling old lava flow presented, for Provin Mountain, save for our presence, was hardly one of the notable climbing venues in the East. The fractured quality of this Triassic rock, in our area, lent itself more to crushing for macadam than to the gymnastic feats that the public has come to associate with high-angle climbing. However, despite such a drawback, this was far-and-away the first of any such telecasts.

9

Not All Hard Work —
Boys Will Be Boys

[KBP] We never saw the need to be despondent about the many issues and problems we faced. Indeed, we had as much fun as possible — even while struggling for our very survival.

One such occasion occurred soon after we separated from WSPR and were consolidating everything on the mountain, where we suddenly became desperately short of office and other working space. The "executive suite," where Bill and I shared a desk, was the alcove/closet originally set aside for AT&T microwave gear, which was mounted high on the wall, above a window that looked down into the studio. The nearby "Traffic office" held two full-time people with desks and a lot of assorted file cabinets and teletype machines in a space that was barely ten feet square, and the only slightly larger "office" next to that was more than fully occupied with the film editors, including their editing benches and storage racks. From that space, all their daily input to the film cameras and control room area had to be carried back downstairs — after first being taken up for them to work on. There was hardly room for people to pass in the hallway. So — poverty or not — William decided we just had to expand.

He looked around outside the building for an area that was more convenient for the film people and would avoid the need to carry their work product upstairs and back down again. Then, conscripting anyone he did not see fully employed at any moment, he cleared a suitable — ten-by twenty-foot — area on the west side of the building adjacent to our iconoscope film cameras, where he could smash a hole in the outside wall to give those people much easier access, and also thereby free the space upstairs for additional offices. The several yards of concrete floor were duly poured and screed smooth by numerous "volunteers." Then Jim Ferguson promoted a truckload of lumber and cinder blocks from the A[delard] Boilard Building Supply Company, and one weekend was devoted to building the outside walls of our first addition.

To "fast forward" some 30 years, before the two of us left our mountain for the last time in the late spring of 1984, we had almost completely (all but about ten linear feet) surrounded the original 60- by 68-foot building with masonry additions, a good part of which labor was done by staff "volunteers," directed and inspired by strawboss Bill and later by Bob Vadnais.

(My William loves maps, claiming they're the most useful wallpaper he knows of, and the hallways of WWLP came to be adorned with Geological Survey topographic sheets of all the areas we cared most about. On one later occasion, when Bill and George Townsend were planning for WRLP, and as another and much larger addition was also in the works at WWLP, they needed a map of part of southern New Hampshire to take with them on a day's outing to the north. One wall of the traffic office was due to come down in the fulfillment of this second WWLP expansion and that wall happened to be adorned with the appropriate map of the day. So, Bill entered, asking Betty and her assistant to stand back while he took his axe and chopped out a large piece of the plasterboard wall; then he and George drove off to the north with their trophy.)

After the walls of the new editing room were up, William determined that we were ready to install the roof, which was to be an extension of what was essentially flat and covered with tar and gravel, but pitched slightly down to the west. We knew we had to have a period of fair weather, as the downhill side of the roof would have to be opened for him to tie the addition's rafters in and get everything watertight again. Relying strictly on the station's weatherman, we were given the okay for a two-day window of sunshine in early April of 1955 and he tore open the appointed part of the eaves trough to provide a ledge onto which the 2 × 10 rafters could rest.

(John Quill, our "springtime" weatherman, was something else. He came to us as a potential engineer, but really only wanted to be a weathercaster. Once we had to take down a cinder block wall, get a concrete floor poured in the area adjacent to our main studio and have everything shipshape for my show by 1 P.M. Very early on the appointed day, Bill was there smashing down the wall and getting the debris carted out of the building, but had to stop so Quill could do local weather segments at 0725 and 0825, as allowed for in the *Today* format.

If that cold front catches up with this warm front, it's gonna rain hard, according to John Quill.

At 0730, when we were back on the network, Bill tossed him a pair of gloves and asked "Hey, John, could you help me get some of these cinder blocks out of here?"

John, a physical fitness buff, turned back as he was starting a series of laps around the studio, as ordained by the Canadian Air Force fitness program, "I'd love to, Bill, but I have to exercise first.")

All went well, and Bill even nailed down two courses of 5/8-inch plywood, before he was brave enough to have some of the "volunteers" break open the hole in the original outside wall, so that there was internal access to the control room, one step lower. Things looked pretty good as the construction crew went home after sunset. But, during the night, there was a 4-inch fall of new, wet snow, and when morning broke WWLP was faced with an incipient flood — a strange and unlikely event on top of a mountain — for which we were decidedly unprepared.

William faced the matter squarely and whenever we were "on the network" most of the engineers and all the production staff would race out of the Control Room, through the new doorway, up the ladder and onto the roof, where they commenced rolling big balls of the wet snow over the edge of the roof. For many of them, being not much more mature than teenagers, this activity soon developed into a snowball fight, but as the sun warmed things, they were sobered by the imminent and alarming prospect of water cascading through that opening in the roof and hole in the wall down into the trenches of the control room. When I drove up, a bit later than the others, I saw the situation and (like the lady from Philadelphia in the *Peterkin Papers,* though I was born in Pittsburgh) asked why someone had not built a dike of the displaced soil that was outside the new walls, so as to block the meltwater from entering the building. That brought an immediate halt to both the flood threat and the fun, but as soon as the dike was built, the snowball fight resumed.

Providing the practical solution for this untoward event earned me a place of respect — however temporary — and thereafter, I was sought out first whenever there was some catastrophic event that might cause the offender to lose stature — or even his job. As time went on, first thing in the morning, I would frequently find a reception committee, often headed by Lou Marek, at the front door, poised to swiftly usher me off to a private conference, hopefully held before Bill found out about the latest "crime."

Hard Water

Despite the fact that our landlord was the City of Springfield's Water Department, their immense tanks were more than 100 feet vertically below the crest of Provin Mountain, so we could not run a line along the ridge for a water supply, and were reduced to boring a well. Unfortunately, lava is not a very good aquifer, and even after drilling down some 350 feet, we were barely able to eke out a flow of 2 gallons per minute, and even this was unfortunately of a very "hard," and iron-rich nature. We had, at best, a marginal water supply, though some 20 years later, we did run a one-inch water line up the hill from West Street, and were then able to enjoy unlimited amounts of the pure and soft water that our landlord was supplying from the Archean granites and gneisses of the Berkshire Hills watershed. However, our well turned out to be an asset of a nature we did not at first recognize; it was a magnificent ground, far superior to the copper wire mesh that George had originally laid out under the station's lawn. A heavy copper wire, attached at the lower end to a five-pound sash weight, and nestled down into that iron-rich water, turned out to be better than any other mountain-top ground return, anywhere.

◆   ◆   ◆

Tonight

With a little assist from Paul Rittenhouse, in the autumn of 1955, Bill managed to get the major cast from NBC's new late night show — *Tonight*, starring Steve Allen—to come up from New York and originate the program from the Eastern States Exposition (The Big 'E') grounds in West Springfield. This was a big deal for us, and equally well recognized by the other local media — even the "enemy" newspapers, who sent a special photographer over during the afternoon setup. Bill carefully positioned himself between Steve Allen and "Doc" Severinson, while the man took a couple of pictures, and a lot of notes before he left. We all looked forward to a nice piece of promotion, until we saw — the next morning — that our leader had been neatly (in those days before Photoshop) excised from the middle of the picture, leaving the *Tonight* host alone with the band leader.

◆   ◆   ◆

Weekends Off?

As in most broadcast operations, WWLP's regular talent worked Monday through Friday and had the weekends off. That was my schedule, too, though — as a founding shareholder and "part of the management" it was just dandy for the Sales Department to sell a live commercial to the Forbes and Wallace department store for me to do in the 11 P.M. late news on Saturday and Sunday, for which I had to make special eight-mile trips from home. (I like to think that my increasingly vigorous complaints to the rest of the management were what soon got us those two-inch videotape machines.)

But the weekends were also when we broke in younger folk to do the local news and weather, as well as when we had part-timers on camera duty and elsewhere. A couple of these younger and more "heads up" part-timers, Bill Harris and Bill Pepin, outlasted us in the television business, earning their stripes as talent during these weekend episodes, when they would work the Audio controls as well as appear on camera. Pepin did audio while Harris did news on-camera, and during the commercial break after the news, Harris would race up take over audio control, while Pepin donned his tie and went down to the weather set — sometimes running into each other, as they traded off-camera duties for places in front of the cameras.

◆　◆　◆

Talent?

At almost the same time that we were proud to note (internally) that George Townsend had run his "proof of performance" and gotten WWLP its permanent license, William found himself in a unionizing pickle. He had invited NABET Local 13 to WWLP, largely on his father's suggestion, but he saw no good reason to go further with restrictive and expensive employment contracts. Then, one day, he was accosted in the hallway outside our diminutive office by one of our first talent, staff announcer Ray Drury, who had also come from WSPR. Ray liked to read the news on-camera and soon fancied himself in the same league as NBC's then lead newscaster, John Cameron Swayze (1906–1995), star of the 15-minute nightly *Camel News Caravan*. Ray showed Bill a bunch of signed enrollment cards from all of our on-the-air figures except me — Drury had not even approached me to sign — and gave him a copy of the AFTRA talent contract which pertained to that pre-freeze broadcasting behemoth, WBZ-TV in Boston.

William stepped back into our office somewhat crestfallen, with what looked like a piece of dreadful news for our non-profit station, as we then were. He took note of the signature cards and studied the contract, trying to determine what his next move should be. Just about that time, a knock came on our office door. It was Burleigh Brown, our sometime sports reporter. He had been one of the most avid "volunteers" in the new film editing room extension and he introduced himself as the newly elected steward of this putative union. "Bill," said Burleigh, "I wouldn't take that contract too seriously, if I were you. Most of us know you can't afford those pay scales, but somehow Ray thinks you're made of money and he's been pushing the rest of us on this."

William then read further into the WBZ-TV contract and found a clause that said the management had the indisputable right to assign shifts and duties. "Hah!" he muttered to me, "I know enough about labor law that right now I shouldn't do anything that isn't allowed for under this contract. But Drury is off news immediately and gets weekend booth duty." He then worked out a new schedule of talent hours and duties, effective the next day, typed it up and posted it on the wall by the announcer's booth.

Within minutes, an irate, red-faced Drury appeared at our office door; "Putnam, you're a s — t-eating sonofabitch! I quit!"

Drury promptly stormed out of the station building, never to be seen again, and someone else did the news that evening. The next morning, Burleigh again appeared at our door; "Bill, I just wanted you to know that there was an AFTRA local meeting again last night and we voted to go inactive. Can I give you any help with the landscaping work around the mountain this weekend?"

◆   ◆   ◆

Occasional Laughter

On another occasion, in the autumn of 1983, the news wire was heavy with stories about the death of the principal — and legendary — figure behind pro football's famous Chicago Bears, George Halas. Our regular late news anchor was then Norm Peters, whose vanity was such that he refused to wear glasses or use contact lenses, and thus had occasional difficulty reading a TelePrompTer. It became time to introduce Roland Jacobs, who had succeeded Burleigh as our principal sports personality. As WWLP came back to the live studio from a story on tape, Norm squinted into the camera and intoned, "A great Chicago sports figure got laid today — to rest, I mean. Here's Rollie with the details." Rollie, who never lost his composure, completed his segment with a straight face, while viewers across western New England might have noticed a slight tremor in the picture but they could not see (or hear, fortunately) what was being said over the camera headsets or how far into the aisles the other personnel in the studio were rolling.

One of our earliest and more versatile "talent" figures was Edward Hatch, who did segments on our news and was the host of the late afternoon *Uncle Ed's Fun Club*, a program designed to appeal to pre-teens, whom we knew would not only teach their parents how to tune in to WWLP, but would also spread the word in classrooms about the station. His *Fun Club* was an audience participation program including a number of cartoons, and it was opened by Ed pulling open a prop door and striding into the midst of the assembled club members, who were seated on the studio floor. One day, in order to enhance the fun aspect of the opening, Bill obtained a small plastic bowl. Having filled it with water while Ed was donning his uniform for the day, the general manager of WWLP placed the bowl carefully on the top of the door, so that it would dump its contents onto the *Fun Club* host as he emerged to start the show. The kids loved it, and Ed was a good sport about the prank, but he never opened his door again without checking overhead.

I was even coerced into repeating a stunt I had learned as a high school football cheerleader. On a dare from a couple of our cameramen, I did a series of cartwheels diagonally across the studio floor, from one corner to the other. Though often urged — even by Bill — to perform this stunt as an opening for my daily hour, I managed to retain my dignity by not trying a repeat.

On that sad day when our idealistic president, John Kennedy, was assassinated in Dallas, I was in my studio living room set, conversing with the final guest of the day. Bill had heard the loud ringing on the AP newswire machine and tore off the first report of the event (which came in around 1:50 EST), then entered the studio and crawled up to the coffee table, carefully staying out of camera range while waving the first report of the event. "Read it!" he stage whispered, "Kennedy's been shot." I realized that not even he would dare intrude on my live show if it were not of major importance, but naively responded, "Which Kennedy?"

"The president, stupid!" as he shoved the news-wire printout into my hand, not caring any more whether he was seen interfering with my show. Like almost every other station in the country, WWLP rapidly joined our network, which spent the rest of the day covering this lugubrious event.

The Hangover

As soon as our financial condition allowed, Bill and I decided we should hold a clients' party on the mountain. After all, he had put a lot of weekend effort into building beautiful dry-stone walls and grading the terrain so the station grounds were attractive enough to show off. Thus, in mid–summer of 1955, we staged our first reception for all our clients, large and small, where they could mingle with station personnel, consume a few drinks, have a bite to eat and, hopefully, be sufficiently sober by the time they hit the public highways that there would be no untoward events, though one good client managed to take a lot of bark off one of our big hemlock trees with his Cadillac while driving home. These parties became so popular with our sales staff that they were an annual event, despite the damage to the hemlock tree.

Meanwhile, one of our staff engineers, Donald Douyard, had gained some minor fame because of his masterful ability to find the most convenient and least expensive local watering holes whenever our staff would be off doing network or other remote originations, an accomplishment which came very close to costing him his job. However, Don's skill at this questionable "bar checking" accomplishment soon earned him the new first name of Dunc (after the late authority on quality dining places, Kentucky-born Duncan Hines). Don was not our most technically skilled engineer/operator, but he was one of the most gregarious and always a willing "mix-master" when Bill had a masonry building project going.

On the morning after one subsequent festive event, when I arrived on the mountain, I found Bill already picking debris out of the garden beside the front door and sweeping up the parking lot. I went into the building, intending to go directly up to our office, but was immediately surrounded by a deputation from Local 13. I found myself hustled off to the studio control room, where I met Dunc, who was lying on the floor and barely able to maintain his grasp on a bottle of Creme de Menthe, left over from the clients' party the night before and from which he continued to take periodic sips.

"Kitty," said Lou, "please don't tell Bill, 'cause Don could be fired for this. Alcohol isn't supposed to be anywhere near an operating control room. He was here like this when Max and I showed up this morning and we don't dare let him drive home. So we've spoken to Ann, his wife, but she hasn't got wheels to come and get him. What should we do?"

About this time, Don stirred himself from his semi-stupor, though still grasping his green bottle, and slurred, "Kitty, you'll take me home, please! I won't go with anyone but you! But promise me you won't tell Bill."

I wasn't sure how his wife would react, but I agreed to be the chauffeur. And, though I didn't promise not to tell Bill, I did agree to intercede with him, if necessary, so as not to fire the popular though sometimes errant Douyard.

Lou and Max Marek then helped get the super-soused engineer into my car and gave me driving instructions for Douyard's home, which was fortunately only a short distance from the mountain. When I arrived there, Ann, who was naturally wondering where her man had been all night, and what sort of condition he might be in, came out to fetch my passenger. I didn't stay to see the outcome of Don's return home, but I felt that whatever the somewhat outraged Ann said, or did, would probably be sufficient

Studio control; producer/director Marie Gerecht at the switcher, Ron Langevin on audio.

punishment for the crime; after all, no person or thing had been damaged, except for the contents of the green bottle.

Tongue Control

Bill Putnam's editorials were quite frequently the talk of the town. He scheduled them to appear three times a day — before the *Today* show and as a segment in the early and late evening newscasts — with his weekly favorite appearing one extra time on Saturday's late news. As a revealing sign of audience turnover, we found that very few people realized his editorials ran more than once. But when the nasty phone calls came in, he would frequently ask me to handle them. This was good, because he did not mind (to this day) exercising, when off-camera and in no mood to suffer fools gladly, some of the choice vocabulary he had learned years earlier from Joe Dodge.

The late Joseph Brooks Dodge had nothing to do with television. For most of his life, he ran the Appalachian Mountain Club's hut system in New Hampshire's White Mountains, and he was widely known for his numerous mountain rescues; his reestablishment of the now-famous weather station atop the highest mountain in the Northeast; his creative citations from Holy Scripture; his vivid, if generally biologically inaccurate, anatomical references; and his plentiful distortions of Noah Webster's dictionary. William's first paying job had been working in the mountains for Joe (at five dollars a week and "all found") and he learned a lot from that "old man of the mountains," mostly — Bill still says, though I tend to differ — "about how to get by with very little, and fix something that has broken with even less."

I had to agree that one of Bill's best routines was his occasional bestowal of a "Half a Horse Award." For this purpose he obtained a 1/20th scale plastic horse and carefully sawed off the front portion, discarding it. Then he mounted the remainder on a wooden base, after which he painted the entire creation to look as if it were brass. If some public figure had done something monumentally or predictably stupid, William would prepare and deliver a suitable description of the offending act while a second studio camera would show a close-up view of this special prop. He would also announce the recipient's name, often with his rate of pay and time on the job. These events were all but unanimously well-received in our area, and excited a great deal of comment, but no awardee ever came up to the mountain to claim the prop.

On another occasion, after we had built "my" station in Dayton, we were attending the annual NAB convention in Chicago, and I took the occasion to arrange a dinner in one of the private rooms of the giant Conrad Hilton Hotel for all of the people from both our stations who were in attendance. As the dinner was winding up, I noticed that the chief engineer of WKEF was sitting quite erect, but had his eyes closed and was occasionally nodding.

It came time to pay the check, which Bill took care of with his company credit card, and then—arranged by a series of hand signals—we all quietly arose and exited the room, leaving the sleepy, but still upright, engineer at his place. When the room was suddenly quiet, Harold opened his eyes to find himself alone, with a number of us out in the hallway, giggling.

◆   ◆   ◆

Pine Cones

The three networks were in the custom of arranging their annual affiliates' meetings on successive spring weekends, mostly in Los Angeles. Partly this was a convenience to the functionaries of multiple station owners, of which there were many, but ABC was a frequent exception to the custom, as one of their five owned stations was in San Francisco. When we were in the wooing stage of our relationship with ABC in Dayton, we made special plans for several of us to attend both NBC and ABC meetings with one set of plane tickets to the coast. Since the formal meetings lasted only four days, this allowed the principal executives of our stations some time to work closely with the Hollingbery people's West Coast offices, as well as for Bill to meet with some of his mountaineering friends in places like Yosemite Valley.

He never took me to the celebrated Ahwanee Hotel in "the valley," as Yosemite is apparently known around the world to high-angle climbers, but on one occasion, he and I drove south from San Francisco to Los Angeles along the very scenic Coastal Highway #1. Half an hour before we approached San Simeon, he saw a sign that said something about Nacimento and suddenly veered off the pavement to climb a forest road some thousands of feet up from the ocean into the mountains.

"What's up here?" I asked, as soon as I realized we were significantly off the beaten track.

"Pine cones," he replied, "great big ones."

The road wound around in an impressive series of switchbacks until finally, at the height of land leading over into the Hunter-Liggett Military Reservation, Bill stopped the car and commenced prowling through the forest in search of any cones that might have fallen from the unique pine trees native to this region and altitude. "These trees," he told me, "were named after the Irish botanist/medical doctor/explorer Thomas Coulter (1793–1843), one of your people, Mother." But he also said that if Sir Isaac Newton had been sitting under one of them — rather than a domestic apple tree — "Gravity, would never have been invented. Sir Isaac would have been killed outright, not merely bopped by an apple."

"How come you knew about these things?" I naively asked.

"I haven't spent all these years as an advisor to the National Forest System for nothing," he responded, "I've got maps of almost every National Forest in the country, and Chief Ed Cliff himself told me about this place." (Bill stayed on that national committee until his reappointment came up in 1972, when, though he was advised by our friend, Senator Brooke, that his reappointment was assured, Bill soon found out that his editorials had earned him a place of distinction — on Nixon's famous "Enemies List." The National Forest System was the loser in that fiasco.)

So we collected a half dozen of the cleanest among these huge and heavy pine cones, which we carried on down to Los Angeles as souvenirs of our trip and to give to some friends at NBC. Unfortunately for one of my party dresses, the pitch from a couple of these cones got onto nearly everything in our car. Though we have returned several times to this area, in subsequent years, and collected many more of these massive and handsome pine cones as gifts for our children and grand-children, I still hate them.

A Swimming Pool

I thought this would be a great adjunct to my show — and so it was, ultimately — but our first attempt at construction was to have Jim Ferguson's boys swap advertising for an above-ground, four-feet-deep, plastic job, which we erected to the west of the station, down near the tower's outer northwest guy anchor. However, on my very first use of this pool, by a burly swimming instructor from Springfield College, he pushed off from the side and the pool's wall collapsed, creating a considerable local flood, as well as a sudden and unexpected end to that segment of my show. Back to the drawing boards.

The next venture was a several-week, lunch-hour project to excavate a deeper hole in the same vicinity, which Bill and the troops then lined with cinder blocks, later reinforced with poured concrete. This excavation was accomplished with the help of some dynamite, which Bill somehow managed to obtain (and on the niceties of whose handling he had learned much while in the Army). However, in the course of blowing out one stump, we almost lost our dear treasurer, when Roland failed to respond sufficiently swiftly to the warning cry of *"fire in the hole!"* When this project was finally completed properly, I always did "remotes" from this pool, because it was sufficiently far from the studio that our camera cables could not easily reach the distance. This swale also became a focus for company parties, only a few yards down from the employees' parking lot. On such occasions, Holly Low, our national sales manager and an avid fisherman, would sometimes find the means to stock the unchlorinated water with trout.

10

Onto the National Scene

[KBP] The year was 1976 and the movement to recognize the potential and value of women in management as well as in politics was gaining momentum throughout the nation. Having found that his vigorous advocacy of UHF-TV had made him more than merely controversial in some circles of broadcasting and thus a lost cause himself, Bill suggested I put my name forward for election as a member of the Television Board of the National Association of Broadcasters. When the votes were counted that year, the vice-president of Springfield Television — me — had come in seventh for the six seats available; but a number of our highly placed friends, including Pete Kenney of NBC and his Washington counterparts, Gene Cowen at ABC and Bill Small at CBS, all urged me to keep at it. Dawson "Tack" Nail, by far the most incisive and trustworthy of the trade press reporters, who always ferreted out everyone's deepest secrets, spread the word on how close I had come (only three votes), and warned the industry that the woman's day was dawning and that I would very likely be back. He advised that the industry would be smart to welcome me.

The following year, the convention was in Houston, hometown of Jack Harris, one of the most farsighted of the industry leaders, one of Bill's friends, and a widely respected former chairman of the NBC TV affiliates. Everyone knew I had Jack's tacit endorsement, as well as that of Bob Ferguson, the current chairman of our network's affiliates, who even endorsed me publicly at one gathering. The Hollingbery staff had been passing out campaign buttons for me and urging all their station owners to vote for me. On the evening when the voting was concluded, I was tired from visiting all the hospitality suites and glad-handing with everyone that anyone knew, so I was abed when the polls were finally closed.

The phone beside my head soon rang me awake; it was George

Mitchell, our Dayton station manager, who had been my producer-director for several prior years. "Kathryn, you've won!"

"How do you know that, George?"

"It was simple. I've spent the last hour or so hanging around outside the polling booth listening to station owners talking as they went in and out. Everyone was talking about their election preferences — 'I'm gonna vote for Harry, Pete, and the girl,' or 'Joe, Jack and the girl.' "Kathryn, you're the only 'girl' and on everyone's list."

"But George, they don't even know my name."

"Don't worry about that, Kathryn; they will very soon."

Apparently I had won overwhelmingly. At my very first board meeting, which was soon held back in Washington at the NAB headquarters on N Street, one radio broadcaster, who had been a longtime fixture in industry politics, told me, "Well, Kitty, I guess I've got to clean up my act and get some more socially acceptable jokes."

"You don't need to worry about that, Jack," I replied, "I've already heard them all."

After a few sessions, with both Radio and Television Boards meeting jointly, even though I was pleasantly accepted in every way, I did find one cause for complaint. Following the midmorning break, forty-four men would troop off to the men's room, which shared a common wall with the ladies' room, which I had all to myself, and I could hear the debates still going on and potential votes being discussed. So, when the courtly South Carolinian, Wilson Wearn, gaveled the joint board meeting back to order one day at 10:30, I raised my hand.

"Yes, Kathryn?"

"I'd like to move that we limit all debate to the formal sessions."

There was a long silence before Wilson announced that he would take the matter under advisement, but thereafter the unofficial men's room–only debates were more subdued.

During my first year on the Television Board, I assumed the traditional role of a "back-bencher" and stayed out of any leadership activity. However, it must have been an eye-opening experience for many on that board when it became obvious that — unlike several others — I did not have to place a phone call before taking a vote. Bill and I had always enjoyed such a high degree of mutual confidence that I knew what our company's position would be on any issue without prior consultation. A year later, when the NAB's Television Board convened, the first order of business was to elect a new chairman. Every other board member now knew that I was my own person and since I was apparently the only member that had no competitors among the crowd, I was elected by acclamation and went up to the dais to take my new seat and the gavel.

At this point, one board member in the back of the room raised his hand. "Kathryn! How do you want to be addressed?"

"Well," I thought for a moment, "the job you've just elected me to has always been called 'Chairman' and I guess that's good enough for me."

"Thank you, Madam Chairman." The questioner then reached into his pocket and handed a dollar bill to his neighbor. The next evening, I had the great pleasure of leading my fellow directors to a White House reception, where I was able to have a few private words with President Gerald Ford, who wanted to ask me about how I felt, as a mother, about the matter of excessive violence as seen on television.

Set Control

The major issue of the day, for television broadcasters, was the never-to-be-resolved issue of how to "protect" children from the impact of adult-only late-night programming. I, being the only mother at large in the hierarchy of the industry, was a most logical spokesman on behalf of broadcasting — which may have been a factor in my unopposed election as chairman, and soon resulted in my being asked to serve as president of the Television Information Office, an organization somewhat akin — in purpose, anyhow — to the Anti-Defamation League of B'nai Brith.

Before that happened, however, I was drawn — willy-nilly — into the public fight over who should control the television set at home. I contended — and still do — that this is a matter of parental responsibility, which cannot (or should not) be subcontracted to others. Bill always told anyone at his home: "as long as I pay the taxes here and the electric bill, I will be the ultimate decider of what is shown on that TV set." Furthermore, I knew that our children (like most youngsters) were smart and clever enough to circumvent any "v-chip" device that someone might install, so we were going to lose anyway, if we relied on something mechanical rather than inculcating good manners and good taste into our children.

Along the way, though, in my capacity as chairman of the Television Board, I was party to a printed debate in *Newsweek* on the subject.

Control (and content) of the TV set was a topic with which Bill and I had considerable experience, and were fully up to speed. As the most visible spokespeople for free-to-the-viewer, over-the-air television in Western Massachusetts, we had both been involved in countless discussions from private cocktail parties to public forums. Bill tended to be the more argumentative, as he is to this day, and he would often deputize me to handle PTA meetings and such, while he would take on the more formal attempts to browbeat television executives, many of which — he used to growl to me — were led by unrealistic, quasi-religious "do-gooders" mostly out to make a name for themselves tilting against a windmill that was too far out of their reach, anyway.

Bill would often point out that his daughter, Kate, had (at age ten) spoken to him about a program we were considering not renewing for use on our air: "Daddy, that's junk!" He would also gladly note that his now distinguished father was "corrupted" by Dead-eye Dick, and that he had been "corrupted" by the then evolving medium of radio. Now there was a new social villain — television. He also did not like debating things with those he felt were bigots or idiots, for they always brought any such discussion down to their level of intelligence.

But the hope for the new medium, in the minds of many would-be reformers, was cable. They were sure that this offshoot of television had enormous promise for the enhanced "quality programming" they were sure could thus be delivered. With the various Discovery Communications, Inc., channels, some of that "promise" is actually being made available to the people, but a lot of the great hoopla for cable (and satellite) television has turned out to be reruns of, or expansions on, what the various would-be reformers did not like in the first place. We tried to tell people, every way we could, that good television programming was expensive to produce, and without the means of supporting such an expense, what many critics, well-meaning and otherwise, of our industry wanted just wasn't going to be delivered — ever.

◆   ◆   ◆

The Smaller Shots

In the mid–1970s Bill and I decided that, while everyone was always willing to wine and dine the big shots in Congress and at the FCC, it was always their underlings who actually took care of issues and problems. Maybe taking some of them to dinner would be a useful and well-received gesture. Thus we arranged, with the help of our Washington-based corporate counsel, Martin Firestone, to have the entire facilities of the Broadcasters' Club, across 17th Street from the Mayflower Hotel, for an evening, and did so for several subsequent years.

By throwing this party for congressional staff people in Washington, we established a second "first," for we had often invited the key personnel from our local competition — print, radio and TV — in Springfield to spend a summer evening on the mountain, where we would arrange a

Kitty with her occasional co-host, Ed Leahy. Bill was explaining his crystal ball ("cracked, cloudy and out of round") — a massive piece of clear quartz he had brought home from near a mountaintop in British Columbia.

buffet meal and bar. Bill had determined that competing with each other did not mean that we had to be mutually hateful. Some of them turned out to be pretty nice folks, and the community we all served was the real winner.

◆　◆　◆

Of Cakes and Dogs

I like to cook! Even now, in my dotage, I enjoy preparing meals for my daughter, Erica, and her family when we visit her back in Massachusetts. But Erica is a dog person, who likes to live with animals in her house — right now there are two cats and one dog — and she has passed this trait on to her daughter, Flynn, an award-winning equestrienne who is planning a post-college career in some sort of work with animals. But animals have their drawbacks in civilized human society.

At one point, Bill gave Erica a female malamute puppy, which was promptly named Chugach. I still think there was an ulterior motive behind that gift, because he couldn't keep a dog in his household in Springfield and Chugach thereafter accompanied Bill to the mountains with great regularity. But malamutes, besides being strong, friendly, loyal and mountain-smart, are also inveterate thieves and they particularly cherish any foodstuff that smells to them of protein.

Anyhow, one Saturday, while Chugach was supposedly in residence at or near my house, I prepared three different kinds of pie for future display on the air, and left them to cool on a table outside the back door, while I went about other weekend household tasks. An hour or so later, I returned to the kitchen and looked out to check on my pies. They had all disappeared, but Erica's dog was lying in her favorite cool spot in the shrubbery, with three empty pie plates scattered nearby.

Malamutes are supposed to be "working dogs" — they pull sleds, the heavy freight of Alaskan lore, as has been well recorded in the works of the late Robert William Service (many of which Bill is still able to recite from memory) — but Chugach was apparently a frustrated retriever. One day she returned home carrying a plastic bag full of used diapers, which she had found on a neighbor's back porch. Another time she brought something more to our liking, a grocery bag full of frozen rock Cornish game hens. I would have liked to keep the latter, but I also wanted to keep my neighbors, and so Erica was dispatched, as soon as she returned home from school, to find out which neighbor was expecting an as-yet-unfilled order of frozen Cornish game hens.

Though the adjacent City of Springfield had a leash law ordinance, that mattered little to a malamute, and tying up such a strong beast was a fruitless endeavor. Chugach soon figured out how to migrate across the nearby Forest Park to Bill's residence in the city. En route home, she was accused of stopping off near the park's famous duck ponds to pick up any unwary bird that happened to be standing on shore (anxiously awaiting capture, no doubt). I was told that those ducks were tough and stringy, but anyhow, Chugach never brought one of them home.

But malamutes were not the only villains my cookery had to contend with. There were two-legged food thieves at large on the mountain — at least, when the goats had left, there was no one else to blame for the bad things that sometimes happened overnight in my corner of the studio.

I once prepared a sponge cake, a real one, complete with chocolate frosting, just like the one I almost had on my disastrous first day, and put it in my studio freezer, for use (hopefully) in the following afternoon's program. Then, an hour or so before air time, when I went to get it out of the freezer, there was no cake. Obviously someone on the night crew had enjoyed a fine dessert, but I was missing a key item for my program. So, I found a real sponge under the sink and covered it with chocolate frosting, placing it on my serving table. It looked as good as its predecessor and was a fine fake, but when I put it back into the freezer at the end of the show, unfortunately it stayed there — clearly untouched — for many weeks, while I wished vainly that the same hungry member of the night crew would try to eat it.

Some among the night crew engaged in other annoying, but non-serious thefts, often rummaging in the open space under my "secretarial" desk and causing the disappearance of various small items I saved there, which I felt I might need for my show in case of any "no-show" guests. The ever-practical William growled a lot about these annoying disappearances and finally decided to try identifying the culprit.

He borrowed a smallish trap, one that perhaps might be good for catching a "fisher cat," from one of his fish cop friends and set it in the space under my desk, where the typewriter would have been, had it ever been put away (which it never was, because "two-fingered Bill" — who still does not know QWERTY—used it as much as I did). "Hah!" he smiled, "Now we'll find out who comes to work with a couple of fingers in a cast."

I was worried about the vigor of Bill's attempt at sleuthing, and I also feared my toes might be victimized by this device, but he was unmoved. The thief must be captured! So, I squealed on him, to his father, one day, and Gregor took my side. A man-trap was a bit much, he stated. Perhaps we'd do better, and be a lot less worried about potential legal actions, if we just put a lock on our office door.

◆ ◆ ◆

Setting the Standard

When we gave Bill Rasmussen the charge of revamping our News (and Information) Department, Bill told him there were only a few absolute ground rules that pertained.

1. Our news was to always meet the masthead standard of the *New York Times*—"All the News that's Fit to Print"; he didn't want our news to be dominated by what he called the "cheap and easy stuff"—bombastic loudmouths, car wrecks, house fires and murders.

2. He wanted us to focus on the positive, and on the matters and events that were more difficult to explain, but in the long run, more important to the public.

3. Bill also mandated that if we were going to mention an upcoming event (like a baseball game) that might be carried on television, even—especially—someplace other than WWLP, we should not be afraid to say where and when. He wanted people to look on our news coverage as factual and thorough—reliable, even if it could not be promotional. "People who really want them are going to find those things, anyhow, whether we tell 'em or not, but then they'll recall that we told 'em so, and our improved credibility is what really matters."

11

Editorials in the "Fairness" Era

[WLP] In its infamous "Mayflower" decision of 1941 (since rescinded), the Federal Communications Commission relied on the scarcity (of useable radio frequencies) concept to mandate that any licensee which allows for the expression of someone's opinion must find a way to give "equal" (later replaced by "comparable") opportunity for the expression of opposing points of view. This became known as the Fairness Doctrine, and it quickly caused every licensee to forgo or forbid the expression of any licensee opinions, or if it did allow them, to advocate only application of the Ten Commandments, the Golden Rule, and homemade apple pie — all under proper formal supervision. After forty years of bureaucratic enforcement "by intimidation and raised eyebrow" of this dubious doctrine, the FCC gave it up because it finally and officially found that the doctrine's enforcement tended mostly to suppress news and chill free speech. In the meantime, the bureaucrats had a tough time with me, because I cited some of their other rules and policy statements, repeatedly pointing out exactly what the FCC later ruled was, in fact, the fact.

The commission also insisted that every licensee had a definite obligation to seek out and give time to any "unmet needs" in its community of license. Thus WWLP was in a bit of a quandary, for the other TV licensee in our immediate area had been owned for many years (in various proportions) by the same folk who owned all the local daily newspapers — the *Hampshire Gazette*, the *Holyoke Transcript*, and the *Springfield Union/News* (later to revert to its time-honored name of *Republican*). If they gave expression to any point of view, we were obligated — under one criterion — to give voice to the opposite. On the other hand, according to the Fairness Doctrine, if we allowed a statement of opinion on our air (other than in a legitimate newscast) we were obligated to give the famous "equal time" to any opponent, which, of course, generally included those who had already gotten a good crack at influencing the public via the local print media. Whatever we did could easily be interpreted as wrong, and WWLP was called on the carpet more than once by FCC staff bureaucrats who were more intent on judging us in the vacuum of our own programming, rather than in the context of the community to which we were licensed.

On one visit to the FCC offices, I ran into Leonidas Polk Bills Emerson, whose glorious name came down from Leonidas Polk (1806–1864), an Episcopal bishop and friend of Jefferson Davis, who was killed leading his regiment in the Civil War. Lonny was then chief of the Office of Opinions and Reviews (a big-time bureaucrat, but I had known him when he worked as a peon for McKenna and Wilkinson) and he advised me that, at long last, the Broadcast Bureau was going to designate WWLP's license renewal application for a public hearing, due to multiple and long-standing complaints about violations of the Fairness Doctrine. However, the spark for Lonny's statement was the fact that we had recently filed under oath (though later amended) an FCC employment report form mistakenly using the same criteria that the Equal Employment Opportunity Commission required of all broadcasters, which were slightly different from those promulgated by the FCC — and had thus overstated the number of female executives in Springfield Television's employ. Why two branches of the federal government had to use different standards as to who counted as an executive, was (and still is) beyond me, though the idiocy of such bureaucratic overplay would be a great topic for a tea party.

Standing there in the fifth-floor hallway, I then advised Lonny, whom I had known for many years, that when this hearing was held, Springfield Television would present only one witness — its president. The same then being Kitty, who had also just been elected chairman of the National Association of Broadcasters Television Board and was thus the foremost female executive in the entire industry. There were also no females on the FCC itself or on its staff hierarchy. Lonny assumed, wrongly, that the "one witness" would be me. Then I told him, "Lonny, I'm really gonna enjoy this hearing, 'cause you guys on the FCC staff are going to look like the biggest and dumbest fools in all of bureaucracy." He then looked further into the matter and persuaded his associates that there was no need for any such proceeding.

We learned to work around the Fairness Doctrine, which was anything but fair to the community, by carefully selecting the targets that might generate a legitimate demand for "equal time." On one occasion, the police officers in the nearby town of Easthampton gave me a tidbit of official abuse by the local fire chief, who was of great political influence in that town and was now urging the selectmen to put his firemen into the same pay category as the cops. The cops didn't like that idea at all, and supplied me with visual evidence that the fire chief had badly dented his official car, when not on official business. So I mentioned this event in one editorial, whereupon Chief Robert Ulm hired a lawyer to sue me for defamation — presumably he felt that form of rebuttal would be better than getting into an "equal time" fracas with me, and figured that — given whatever facts were involved — he would come out better in a court of law than the court of public opinion. Or maybe he was more intent on slapping me down a peg — I never knew.

So exactly one day after the chief had gotten a big splash in the local press for announcing he was going to sue me for all manner of damages, WWLP reran the offending editorial, in full, and I prefaced it by stating that we did so, "just to be sure everyone knows exactly what I said and what Chief Ulm's lawsuit is all about." Very soon, his lawyer was questioning me in deposition, and I pointedly refused to name any sources for the information I had broadcast. Everyone knew my source had to be within the Easthampton Police Department, but I was not about to confirm that as fact, thereby protecting the cops from any reprisal at the hands of Easthampton's controlling political power. Being threatened with going to jail if I failed to answer, I rather looked forward to the process, since the sheriff/proprietor of the Hampshire County jail was an old and dear friend; I would also look like a journalistic hero for protecting my underdog sources.

One evening, while the case was pending, the selectmen of East-hampton were motivated to convene a public hearing into the matter, which had created quite a local buzz since my multiple whammy at the fire chief. So, I drove there and found my way inside the crowded town hall. With my appearance in the back of the room, there began to arise numerous cries of "He's here! He's here! Ask him to speak!" But Ulm's minions on the dais didn't want any of that, so my presence was officially ignored.

Unfortunately for my trip behind bars, I was soon advised by Dudley Wallace, a wise old lawyer on Springfield Television's Board, "Bill, not that we don't trust Kitty to run things well, but you don't really want to go to jail. Wasn't there anyone else you talked to about this matter before you aired it?"

"Yes, several, as well as most of Easthampton's Police Department, but I'll never say that on the record."

"Have any of the others died since you spoke to them?"

"Only Gene Graves, the volunteer fire chief in Whately, and I met with him, at his diner on Route 5, when preparing to air the matter. Gene used to serve up an excellent breakfast, along with a good bit of valuable gossip; I always stop there when I'm going upcountry or to WRLP."

"Well, just name him, Bill; he won't mind."

So I told Ulm's lawyer I had talked with Gene Graves, and the deposition soon became as dead as Gene. The matter then came up for trial in the Superior Court of Northampton, and on the appointed day, the Hampshire County sheriff, the late Johnny Boyle, who ran the most progressive jail in the state, with a nationally envied low rate of recidivism — as we had frequently noted on the air — appeared in the courtroom, dressed in his most impressive official finery, to give me a grand public handshake and welcome. Before court began, he took me to the window of the second floor courtroom and pointed out a bunch of men working on the lawn and sidewalk outside. "Those are my boys, Bill; I give them this opportunity to earn a bit of money and get some fresh air. A couple of them will have lunch today with their girlfriends."

"Have any of your prisoners ever taken off from one of these outings?"

"Nope. I don't think any of them would ever want to spoil a good thing."

The actual trial was over almost before it began. After the fire chief's lawyer rested his case in less than one hour, the judge turned to the jury and directed them to find me innocent — not one of the chief's lawyer's allegations had merit or any relationship to the charge made against me — and ended with "... and a good day to you, Mr. Putnam." Ulm soon took a similar job at the other end of Massachusetts. This was the grand finale of my career in editorials, but there had been several noteworthy ones.

One of my favorite targets was the state legislature, or "General Court" as its Lower House is called in the Massachusetts Constitution. Unfortunately, beating up on legislators is somewhat akin to shooting fish in a barrel, though I did have a few respected personal friends there, such as Tony Scibelli and Alan Sisitsky, of which the former was a semipermanent fixture, becoming the doyen of the legislature. However, we felt there

WWLP's third Miss Romper Room — Janet (Burke) Dunham.

might be cause for an occasional rebuttal comment and, in order to keep
our skirts clean with the FCC, I arranged for written copies of all my editorials to be sent once a week to the Speaker's Office in Boston (almost
100 miles distant from the mountain, where we did not have any signal,
and thus many of the state representatives from our area might not actually
be able to hear any particular commentary on their behavior). This led
to a long-lasting — to this day — friendship with a true rarity in Massachusetts politics, the progressive and idealistic speaker, David Michael
Bartley, whose home district included much of Holyoke.

One of our Miss Romper Rooms, Janet Burke, later married NBC's
lawyer, Corydon Dunham, and we would meet at periodic affiliates' gatherings, so I got to know her husband, with whom I maintained communication after we had left broadcasting. Cory, in his retirement, has taken
up a cause that I touched on in an earlier book on the German-born
printer, John Peter Zenger (1697–1746), who went to jail in defense of
the freedom to publish the truth — the primal founding father of the

famous American First Amendment. Cory's latest opus, after a couple that led up to the topic, is on how the FCC and government collectively attempt to censor any news its functionaries do not like — from presidents down to fire chiefs.

In the fall of 1957, Springfield was to hold its first election under a new "Strong Mayor" charter, which WWLP had campaigned for, and the incumbent under the old charter, Thomas J. O'Connor, was being strongly supported by the Springfield newspapers, which even ran front-page editorials extolling his virtues. This gave me a target, other than the incumbent, so I looked into the public records to determine what favors O'Connor might have done to warrant such unusual and favored treatment, and I found that the mayor had been in the custom of declaring

Bill Putnam reading a viewer complaint letter. When no one else would do a hard-hitting editorial, Bill took over the job personally.

an "emergency" whenever he wanted to put some deserving friends on the public payroll for a week or two. According to this loophole in Massachusetts Civil Service law, in case of "emergency," the normal rules about hiring through Civil Service procedures are suspended until the crisis has been dealt with. In looking over the public records in the city hall, I found there had been emergencies because of "heavy snow," when the streets were dry; emergencies for a "flood," in the midst of long, dry spells and several similar, grossly transparent, abuses. Most of these payroll-padding exercises had been done at the expense of the Park Department (where perhaps these nonworkers could readily hide among the trees).

I also found that property tax assessments had been dramatically reduced on several newspaper-owned properties in the City of Springfield. All this made for several juicy reports, during which I found a way to explain the reasons for the unusual front-page political endorsements. Though offered an opportunity, the then proprietors of the Springfield newspapers did not deign to reply on WWLP, which — remember — had managed to go on the air in 1953 without their noticing it. Naturally, O'Connor wanted equal time — which we were happy to arrange; but, unfortunately for him, we were then explicitly obligated, under other FCC regulations, to provide similar time to his opponent.

The result of this process was that WWLP had to expand the slots wherein we ran the editorials. It made for a several-week electronic Donnybrook — [1] Putnam, [2] O'Connor and then [3] the challenger, Charles Vincent Ryan, Jr.,— each for two minutes. But the political result was astounding, as well as a bonanza for our local Sales Department, which soon experienced a quantum jump in revenue — it never again had to explain the relative power of WWLP on Channel 22 to influence the public. Of the 62 voting precincts in the city of Springfield, Ryan carried 60 — the largest political landslide in the city's history.

A few years later, when Ryan was perceived as having been an excellent mayor, he decided to run for Congress in a Democratic primary fight against the incumbent in the 2nd District of Massachusetts, Edward Patrick Boland. However, Boland had also been an exemplary public servant and we backed him with equal vigor; he won handily and was never challenged again.

There were other sequels, one of which was particularly rewarding, personally.

After we had sold the stations, I was appointed to Springfield's Park

Commission by Mayor Mary Hurley, and promptly elected its chairman. In the four years of my tenure (before resigning to move to Flagstaff) I was many times complimented by permanent employees of the department for having exposed, and thus ended, a problem which had bothered them as much as it did the taxpayers.

Soon after this drubbing of the newspapers' political influence, the tangled ownership mess that Sherman Bowles had left behind him finally awakened all the other heretofore silent shareholders of his great-grand-father's newspaper legacy, and it was all sold to Samuel Irving Newhouse (1895–1979) soon afterwards. The local Newhouse representative was David Starr, with whom we soon began to enjoy a high measure of cordiality that lasts to this day. Some years later, before his death, Tom O'Connor and I became reconciled, and he was one of the last elected commissioners of Hamden County.

Over the many years of our stewardship, Kitty and I made up for

"Servants of the Public" dinner and salute to Bill Putnam. Ed Kennedy, Mayor William Sullivan, toastmaster Gerry McCarthy (back to camera; president of the local AFL-CIO), Edward P. Boland, Caroline J. Putnam.

some of my unwanted, though accurate, commentaries by holding an annual recognition party and award ceremony on the air for those people — on the public payroll — whom we signaled out for commendation as Outstanding Servants of the Public. There were quite a few of them, from all around the region. And once, they got together and threw a party for me.

12

Dealing with the FCC

Policy vs. Practice

[WLP] The Federal Communications Commission has a number of high-sounding clauses in its "organic act" of 1934, which dictates general policy concerns and the like. High among them is the no longer often-cited Davis Amendment (the 1928 creation of Rep. Ewin Lamar Davis of Tennessee), which mandated that all the radio frequencies be equitably distributed among the various states and territories. Then there are periodic decisions and statements of what the current Commissioners believe to be fair interpretations of their duties. Most frequently cited is the fact that broadcasters are supposed to always adhere to the everywhere vaguely defined *"public interest, convenience and necessity"* as a part of their license to use "the public's" airwaves. This frequently quoted phrase first appears in the Interstate Commerce Act of 1887. However, our friend, Commissioner Robert E. Lee, always told broadcasters that their first duty was to make a profit — without which no licensee could ever hope to serve the public interest, and might well become a public burden.

However, all the high-sounding policy statements encouraging the use and evolution of the UHF band came to naught when mouthed by Eisenhower-appointed chairmen of the FCC like Fred Ford, George McConnaughey, and John Doerfer, and carried little value when the Commission was faced with a choice of action involving a well-entrenched VHF firm with big-time lawyers and the right political connections on the one hand, and UHF station owners on the other. WWLP became a prime case in point.

The original local owners of WNHC-TV in New Haven had sold their station to Triangle Publications, owners of the *Philadelphia Inquirer,* the *Philadelphia Daily News,* the *Daily Racing Form,* numerous other FCC licensees, and *TV Guide* — most of which were soon to be acquired by

Capitol Cities Broadcasting, but were then a fiefdom of Walter Annenberg (1908–2002). With the purchase of stations by NBC and CBS in Hartford, WNHC-TV had become a full-time ABC-TV affiliate, and was now licensed to Channel 8, which is electronically adjacent to Channel 7. If it were to move its transmitter a bit farther to the north and east — as well as farther away from its city of license — this would enhance the clear signal area of ABC's flagship station on Channel 7 in New York City. Such a move was asked for, but we could see that this new transmitter site would also beam a strong VHF signal straight upriver into Springfield, as well as diminish the channel's signal strength in New Haven, its "city of license." The FCC, however, was happy to grant this move to a major fundraiser for the Republican Party, its Broadcast Bureau not caring a whit at thus aiming a devastating economic blow at several struggling UHF stations. So we objected, though unsupported by any of the other stations affected, contending this was contrary to a number of the FCC's long-standing policies.

At first, I went to our Washington counsel, McKenna and Wilkinson, the firm my father had selected on the advice of his Washington apartment neighbor and prior associate in the Office of Contract Settlement under President Franklin Roosevelt, ABC vice-president, Robert H. Hinckley (1891–1988). The lawyers demurred; despite taking our retainers for several years, at this critical "moment of truth," Jim McKenna said that their most important client, ABC, forbade them from arguing our side. They pointed us to Seymour Chase, Esq., an independent practitioner.

A hearing examiner (an office soon upgraded to "administrative law judge") was soon assigned to conduct a hearing into the matter and — despite being told that New Haven was the only major city in New England where the steepness of local terrain had mandated a major highway tunnel and that widespread "shadowing" already existed, found, incredibly, that the "Bullington" curves of propagation would overcome such a disability if the station's transmitter site were located farther away. He also gave no weight to the evidence, common and widely known in the industry, even admitted by the FCC, that any UHF stations would suffer from this enhanced VHF competition and that their (our) local service was useful enough to be protected from this sort of abuse. Despite all our protestations and Sy Chase's eloquence, the examiner, not unexpectedly, for he had seemed unfriendly to us all through the hearing, found for Triangle. So we appealed to the full Commission.

Our only moment of pleasure in that hearing had come at the point when one of our witnesses, the spokesman for the Springfield Council of Churches, was asked by the Triangle lawyer, in an attempt to discredit his testimony: "You represent the Council of Churches, but does that mean you are speaking for the Episcopalians?" At this query, the clergyman whipped a letter out of his pocket from the Bishop of Western Massachusetts, the Right Reverend William Appleton Lawrence, Jr., (who happened to share some ancestry with Roger Putnam) and read a sterling encomium about WWLP's service into the record, while the opposing lawyer fumed, unable to object to the clergyman's use of such "hearsay" evidence, because he had asked the question in cross-examination.

It was "make-or-break" day for WWLP when our case came up before the full Commission. But we suddenly got lucky! The FCC normally schedules several cases to be heard and decided at one day's plenary meeting, and the case being argued prior to ours involved an about-to-be-former

Fr. Fidelis Rice, of the Passionist Fathers Monastery in West Springfield, was a regular on Sunday Mass and did a three-hour studio marathon on Good Fridays; John Fergie on camera.

FM broadcaster from Chicago. It turned out that he had been inventively using one of the two side-carriers of his frequency to supply up-to-the-minute horse-racing data to every bar and bistro in Chicagoland — a public service of a sort, but also a terribly bad sin (in those prudish days) for any broadcaster.

Then one day it had all come to an end — the FBI, the IRS, the FCC, the Chicago Vice Squad and numerous other now unremembered agencies and minions of imperialism had collectively descended on all the patrons of his "service" as well as his station, and put everyone out of business. Chase, Townsend and I were sitting in the back of the FCC meeting room witnessing the final act in the tragedy of an FM station. Despite the growing use of lotteries by many churches, fraternal clubs and numerous state governments (including the FCC itself a few years later, when it started awarding hopefully lucrative frequencies by lottery) the full Commission was about to confirm the loss of this man's license and livelihood.

Then one of the seven Commissioners asked a very right, but legally irrelevant, question, "Where did these people get the horse-racing information they broadcast?"

"From Triangle Publications, sir," the FM station's lawyer promptly answered; "they supply it by wire all across the country."

"But this isn't the Triangle case we're hearing now, is it?"

"No, sir, that's the next item on your docket."

With such a lead-in, our victory was assured even before our case came up, and that tower atop Mount Higby was never built; but, as the Newcomen Society used to say: "*Actorum memores simul affectamus agenda*" (by remembrance of the past, we continue to influence the future). Years later, we came to conclude that ABC, which would also have benefitted from the move, had not forgotten.

The Good Commissioner

The Honorable Robert Emmet Lee (1912–1993), whose northwest corner office decor came to include a life-sized picture of his visage staring out from a Confederate Army uniform, was a native of Chicago and had once been an accountant with the FBI. A friend of FBI Director John

Edgar Hoover (1895–1972) and Senator Joseph McCarthy (1908–1957), he was appointed to be one of the "seven wise men" early in the administration of President Eisenhower. I was never able to determine — and never dared to ask — what political aberration had caused him, a Republican with that sort of aegis, to adopt UHF TV as his cause, but adopt us he did, and his patronage encouraged many new station owners and saved a great many existing ones from despair. Commissioner Lee also had a wonderful sense of humor and a very quick wit. As the chief spokesman for UHF issues, I was always welcome in his office, and we came to be personal friends over his 28 years on the Commission.

During some official function, a group of us, including Commissioner Lee, was having lunch together at a restaurant across Pennsylvania Avenue from the then FCC offices. Midway through our meal, a big-time Washington lobbyist appeared beside our table.

"Buy you a drink, Commissioner?"

"No thanks, Mr. _____ (The lobbyist is well-known and, the last I knew, was still at it, and thus shall remain nameless herein.) If it's for friendship, you shouldn't have opposed the Senate confirmation of my reappointment last year. If it's a bribe, one drink is not nearly enough."

At another point, when Kitty was president of the New England Chapter of the American Women in Radio and Television (AWRT, but now renamed to the New Alliance for Women in Media), she asked if I could find a big shot for her annual meeting — to be held in Franconia, New Hampshire. I thought about getting someone from NBC, but had never enjoyed much success there, so I thought better of that and called Bob's office in Washington. He promptly accepted but (since he was a notorious "flat-lander") made me promise that I would be his personal guide through the White Mountain area.

This gathering was also the only time I was able to convince Kitty to have a go at my relaxation hobby of mountaineering. After she had checked in at the Horse and Hounds Inn in Franconia Village (where her meeting was to take place) the warm and sunny autumn day was still young, so I suggested she might wish to join me in an easy rock climb — back up at Franconia Notch, on Artists' Bluff. To my immense surprise, she swiftly accepted and donned a pair of sneakers. A few minutes later she and I found our way to the base of this "beginners' cliff." I tied her into the rope and quickly scampered up the first pitch. Having watched my hand and footholds in attaining the midpoint ledge, the lady — who

Kitty and fellow women broadcasters, with "good commissioner" Bob Lee at the AWRT meeting in Franconia, NH.

always maintained her fighting trim — found it easy to join me. She sat down beside me and looked across the shallow lake to the south. However, before I could assuage her trepidation, and to my considerable discomfort, she unexpectedly experienced the common symptom of all first-time rock-climbers, looking down and experiencing the consequent feeling of dangerous exposure.

"William! William! What have you gotten me into? I've got small children! Get me out of here! Right now!"

This was not the first time I had held her hand, for Kitty and I had long been providing mutual emotional support when our corporate (and occasionally personal) difficulties seemed overwhelming. But up on this cliff, however minor it was in the totality of mountains, it was my milieu, so I had to offer the maximum security in comfort, though she had asked for none of it, only repeatedly sobbing a demand to be once again on flat ground — and soon!

I met the good commissioner's plane at the Lebanon, New Hampshire, airport the next day around noon, while Kitty was conducting her board meeting, and drove him about some of the sights of the area where I had misspent so much of my youth. Since his speech was set for Saturday evening, the day was free, so I asked if he would like to go on a bit of a hike with me. In my avocational persona, I was at that time chairman of the Appalachian Mountain Club's Committee on Mountain Leadership and wanted to see how certain of the club's operations were conducted. So, Mr. Lee and I drove down to Mount Cardigan, where the club had a lodge, and started up the mountain, meeting groups of other hikers along the way. Finally, we attained the rocky, granite area just below the crest of this 3,121-foot eminence. At that point, Bob asked if it was time to use the climbing rope he had seen bulging out of my pack.

Nothing in this world — or the next — would have induced me to cause this man a moment's concern or pain, though the terrain we were on would never have called for a rope under any normal circumstances. But rope up we did, though Bob's idea of climbing technique (which I did not have the courage to correct) was to insist that he had the right, whenever he felt like it, to give a good tug on the rope to help him in his ascent. At last we came to the open area near the summit and sat down to view the puffy white clouds that dominated the eastern sky.

"You know, Bill, I'm no relative of that southern general."

"Yeah. I know that picture in your office is a bit of a joke."

"Once, at some Washington affair, in the mid–1950s, in the late stages of what was once the Solid [Democratic, though conservative] South, I ran into a strongly partisan senator from one of the Southern states who told me: 'You know, Commissioner, I wasn't going to vote to approve your appointment, but then one of my staff reminded me what the reaction might be from my constituents when they learned I had voted against Robert E. Lee.'"

(When Lee's second seven-year term was approaching its end, in late June of 1967, President Lyndon Johnson was dilatory in sending his reappointment up to the Senate, and Bob felt he was being trifled with, so he sent the president a letter (two days before his term was to expire) stating that he would not remain dangling and was going to resign at once. Instead, he got an immediate phone call from the president and was promptly reappointed.)

"My father, Patrick Joseph Lee, came over to this country about the start of this century and landed in Boston. According to what he once told me, there was a bunch of his friends from Garrynagry standing on the front deck of the ship as it came into the harbor. 'Look at those buildings,' cried one of them, and my father, a devout follower of Robert Emmet and hater of all imposed authority, responded, 'If there's buildings there's people, and if there's people there's a givermint, and if there's a givermint, I'm agin' it.'" The good commissioner paused to peer at the distant clouds and I commenced recoiling my rope. "But he soon found a job as a policeman in Chicago and that's what led to my employment with the FBI. You know, Bill, I was trained as an accountant — that's what I did for the FBI — follow the money; and I'd love to have an official reason to get a subpoena and take a real look at the books of those networks."

Bob Lee was much in demand at breakfast meetings of the Knights of Columbus, where his Irish brand of self-deprecating humor went over well. He also became highly respected, indeed loved, by the broadcasters of America — not just we in UHF, but ultimately by all the industry, for, as his decisions on the FCC consistently demonstrated, he did not approach regulation in theory but truly understood what our business was all about and how it worked in practice. However, he was equally serious about applying all aspects of "*the public interest, convenience, and necessity,*" but always tempered it with his strong sense of realism. Though he served on the FCC longer than anyone before or since, he was never its chairman, until the very last few months of his 28th year.

Early in 1981, the trade press (Tack Nail) reported that Lee would not accept another seven-year term on the FCC. At the FCC Question Period, a popular feature of the National Association of Broadcasters Annual Convention, that year being held in Las Vegas, I joined the queue of those who had something to bring to the FCC's attention.

Finally came my turn at the microphone: "My name is William Lowell Putnam. I'm a television broadcaster from western Massachusetts, and I have a matter for Mr. Lee."

The good commissioner stood up.

"Sir, I have come to know you over the many years you have been on this Commission, for it almost matches my years as a broadcaster, which I am sure would have been quite limited except for you. I have worked closely with you, mostly on UHF matters, all these years, and — along with most of those in this room — have always been grateful for your thorough and realistic understanding of the industry your Commission regulates. However, I do have one great and personal regret. I am deeply sorry it has taken so awfully long for me to be able to address you as 'Mr. Chairman.'"

Bob Lee mumbled something no one understood, wiped some tears from his eyes, and sat down. I returned to my seat near Kitty, amid thunderous applause, but also with tears in my eyes, for I knew that television broadcasting was changing and would never be the same when Bob Lee finally retired. A few weeks later, when she and I were at a smaller gathering, a farewell dinner for Mr. Lee in Washington offered by MST, Bob turned to me, "Bill, I guess it must be the mountains that keep you so young-looking, but I'm getting on, you know."

"Perish the thought," I replied, "but I'll always take you to the mountains, whenever you want to go."

"Well, Bill, I know I'm getting on, 'cause every time I bend down to tie my shoe now, I look around to see if there's anything else I should take care of, while I'm bent down there."

While many within the television industry came to regard Newton Norman Minow, a lawyer from Chicago, with considerable suspicion, particularly after his "Vast Wasteland" speech to the annual NAB Convention at the Sheraton-Park Hotel in Washington, on May 9, 1961, during his 26 months as chairman, I always found his office door to be open, and he was generally on the mark with his criticisms. But all that came after I answered his phone call. That speech, by the way, was reported in some of the trade press as "The day the minnow bit the whale" and was widely, if not deliberately, misinterpreted in the print media as a damning disparagement of television. But it contained quite a number of very fair criticisms, with which many of the more idealistic broadcasters agreed. A great deal of television programming — even more now that the nation seems to have gone mostly to cable (or satellite) — is not of a standard or content that many broadcasters feel personally proud to urge their families to enjoy. Over the years, I have been forced to the conclusion that there is a sort of Gresham's Law about television programming, not merely about bad money driving out the good. The taste of the greater part of humanity is not for Shakespeare and Beethoven, but rather for Slapstick and Bennie Hill. And the latter can beat out the former almost any day or time.

"Mr. Putnam, I want to have a talk with you about what the FCC can do to help make UHF television work. How soon can you get to Washington?"

This was the kind of call I had long been praying for, but never fully expected to receive. "Is tomorrow okay?"

I could commence driving south whenever I wanted, and quickly settled on being at Chairman Minow's office at 10:00 A.M., the very next morning. As the call went on, I could see that Kitty's normally happy smile had returned. Maybe our fortunes were finally about to take a substantial turn for the better.

"Well, Mother, dear, I guess you can keep things in order around here without me for as long as the chairman wants to confer. Can you call Andy Kauffman, though, and tell him to find a decent restaurant? I'll be with him tonight. I'm outta here!"

Over the next several hours, as I drove south to spend the evening with my oldest mountaineering friend, Andrew John Kauffman, II (1920–2002), with whom I had made numerous first ascents around North America, who was the authority on French Communists for the Department of State, and who always had a spare bed for me in his Washington apartment, I had ample time to review the alternatives and recent history of the problems affecting UHF television, as well as my own part in trying to get some action. (Andy's lengthy memo in the early 1950s, on the meaning and impact of the return to power of Charles DeGaulle, still reads with chilling accuracy.)

From the time the FCC authorized use of the UHF band, the manufacturers of television receivers had been making two production lines of sets — one that contained a tuner (albeit primitive) capable of bringing in UHF signals — and a much larger production line of TV receivers that cost a few dollars less but could tune only to the 12 VHF channels. They traditionally sold many more of the latter because in most parts of the country, UHF stations either never existed at all, or soon went dark while trying to compete with the earlier stations that could reach every home receiver.

Those stations, like WWLP, which had only one VHF competitor for its first few years, and stations in similar or generally smaller markets, such as Wilkes-Barre, Yakima, Fresno, Bakersfield, Erie, South Bend and central Illinois, had all been clamoring vainly for recognition and help. But, at periodic gatherings, while I was invariably elected Chairman, I

A group of UHF operators convenes on Provin Mountain in the spring of
1957—William L. Putnam, John W. English, Robert M. Stough, Harold
Thomas, John A. Fergie, and Lawrence Turet.

was seldom given much financial (or legal and engineering) assistance
when I would try to get these owners to collaborate in a push for a unified
approach. Our most reliable friend in this effort was the late John W.
English, a prominent lawyer of Erie, Pennsylvania, and a part owner of
that city's CBS affiliate on Channel 33, WSEE-TV. He and I became close
friends, even to the extent that he and his wife, Ottilie, would take in
Erica's malamute, Chugach, when I drove through Erie on my way home
from the mountains, and I could always count on his station sending a
few dollars to help with our intermittent attempts to secure recognition
on Madison Avenue and in Washington.

John English had an immense repertoire of stories about the practice
of law. One that I found most amusing concerned a case that was being
heard on appeal by the Pennsylvania Supreme Court. One side was being
represented by a distinguished trial lawyer named Johnson, who was a
regular in many such appeals. In this case he made his presentation that
a certain set of facts led to a conclusion in favor of his client, but was

stopped by the chief justice with a query: "Mr. Johnson, were you not here before us, just last week, arguing that almost these identical conditions led to the exact opposite conclusion?"

"That is true, sir. But you'll have to agree that in at least one of these instances I have been right."

John also told me of a visit he made, across the lake, to a social gathering in London, Ontario. At this affair, one veddy English gentleman was vigorously declaiming against everything Irish, but was also probing each of the guests in turn about the derivations of their respective names. At last, he came to John and spoke, "Your name is English. It must have a very special origin."

"Oh, it certainly does, sir," replied John. "But you see I'm of Irish ancestry, and as far as I can determine, the first to bear my name was the village ne'er-do-well and he was therefore named for the most odious thing his neighbors and associates could think of."

Over the years, I visited frequently with John and Ottilie in Erie. He and I appeared often before committees of the Congress which had oversight of the FCC, the Interstate and Foreign Commerce Committees of both House and Senate. Mr. Dingell, of Michigan, the perennial chairman of the House Committee, tended to be unsympathetic and often hostile, though his subcommittee chairman with more immediate jurisdiction over communications, Mr. Waxman, was less so, but instead was primarily concerned about his Hollywood constituency. Senators Magnusson (of Washington) and Pastore (of Rhode Island), in the upper chamber, were invariably receptive, polite and friendly; but none of them ever did anything useful for UHF-TV, though Pastore did have a legal connection with a Channel 16 licensee in Providence that had gone dark, early on.

It wasn't that the FCC itself did nothing that was bothersome, it was how the commissioners did it. In 1956, for example, Chairman George McConnaughey organized an official study of the technical viability of UHF-TV, which consisted of representatives from several industry groups: [1] the three networks — ABC, NBC and CBS; [2] the VHF station owners' union [Association of Maximum Service Telecasters — MST]; [3] the manufacturers [Electronic Industries Association — EIA]; [4] the UHF union (such as it was) [Committee for Competitive Television — CCT] — of which the representatives were John English and I, with technical advice from George Townsend; and [5] the Public Broadcasting System. This august body was called the *Television Allocations Study Organization*

In 1959 WWLP brought a special planeload of FCC members and staff from Washington to visit a proudly profitable UHF station. Bill Putnam, at left (Roger behind), explains UHF facts of life to FCC acting chairman, Rosel H. Hyde, while Jim McKenna and FCC engineering staff study pictures at WWLP Master Control (Lou Chenevert, presiding, with visiting airline hostess).

(TASO) and its board met periodically, mostly in Washington. It was headed by an aging (b. 1905) consulting engineer named George R. Town, whose "labors" epitomized that word "delay." I always abstained from voting on matters involving the spending of TASO money, for we in UHF were unable to contribute more than a very little, but John and I never hesitated to speak up and be counted on policy matters and any formal decisions.

At one TASO meeting, successor FCC chairman John Doerfer, suggested it would be wrong to change the audio to video power ratio from 50 percent down to 10 percent. He told the assembled TASO directors, "In my home state of Wisconsin, many people watching television [from Chicago or Milwaukee] have such snowy pictures that they need the higher audio power so as to enable them to continue to enjoy the program during periods when the picture often fades out completely." I refrained from informing him — because it was clearly a waste of effort since the man already had his mind made up about UHF — that if he encouraged the development of UHF, his Commission had already allocated some two dozen channels, similar to that used by the obviously successful WWLP, to communities across Wisconsin (a good many of which were later activated).

I, along with many others, was never able to understand how the FCC had ever felt morally able to allocate 70 channels of space (414 mega-cycles) in the UHF band to television, if it hadn't somehow already deter-mined that this part of the radio spectrum was satisfactory for the purpose. However, during the dark years of the Eisenhower administration and several years after implementing the official decision, it was now necessary to *study* it, though the evidence was already in on all practical engineering concerns (after all, WWLP, even on the exalted frequency of Channel 61, had had its FCC license and "proof of performance" for far longer than most post-freeze VHF stations).

I had given serious thought to formally refusing to have any part of TASO, on the grounds that it was wholly unnecessary and merely a delay-ing mechanism. UHF television was obviously technically quite work-able — the only problems lay in the economic and political decisions we had to live with. But John English convinced me that if we refused to participate we would not create a sufficient splash to be meaningfully effective and would thus end up having no useful input. While no official cared, or dared, to say it publicly, UHF's problems lay in the FCC's Table of Allocations; the problems were solidly bureaucratic, economic and political, never technical. Thus, without ever being officially mentioned, *delay* was the obvious purpose of TASO. As long as nothing was done to change the allocations system, or to require *all* TV sets to be able to receive *all* stations, this huge part of the spectrum would remain basically under-utilized, the defacto monopoly of 108 prefreeze, VHF stations would remain entrenched, with first call on the best network or syndicated offer-ings over any nearby UHF outlets, and the monopolistic revenues would continue to flow. As in the health care debate of 2009 and the subsequent mid–term Congressional campaign, all facts and logic to the contrary were irrelevant, for the moneyed interests commanded the stage of officialdom. Almost every influential element of broadcasting and its regulation — even some of our friends — had been sold on the idea that the "UHF problem" was "technical." No one, however, disputed certain unmistakable facts:

during 1953 and 1954, relying on the FCC's engineering determination that the UHF band was suitable, 156 such stations had gone on the air, but there were only 80 left at the time of my private meeting with the new chairman.

I rehearsed all this with Mr. Minow, though I very soon recognized that he had done a fair amount of homework prior to my arrival in his office. He terminated my recitation of history by asking what I would recommend that the FCC do — now.

This was my great moment of opportunity.

"There are two routes you could take, sir. Initiate proceedings for widespread de-intermixture of television allocations, so that the VHF stations are concentrated in some areas. Then there will be lots of prosperous islands of UHF."

I recited a few of the specific options around the country, which, because of the way the FCC's Table of Allocations worked out, mostly affected channels numbered 3 and 8. Then I mentioned a longer-term idea; get the Congress to enact a law that forbade shipment in interstate commerce of television receivers that were not capable of receiving *all* the channels allocated to television broadcasting. I told him that my congressman, Eddie Boland [he of the amendment, the violation of which later made Lt. Col. Oliver North infamous], had been introducing such a measure for several years, but it had never been reported out of committee.

Minow liked the second idea, but wondered about the politics of it — how could the Congress become more motivated? Though I would have dearly loved to eliminate the nearest Channels 3 and 8 from my neck of the woods, I was willing to settle in for the long haul. "You propose a lot of de-intermixture, Mr. Chairman, which is totally within your Commission's powers and duties, and my guess is that the Congress will quickly find an All-Channel Receiver Law quite an acceptable alternative."

The All-Channel Bill Hearings

Within a few weeks of my visit with Mr. Minow, the FCC had accepted both suggestions; it announced a proposal whereby a large number of allocations, mostly for Channels 3 and 8, were to be reassigned to different communities and the current holders of such permits given the "unworkable" and/or "second-rate" UHF channels instead. And it also asked the Congress to enact the suggested law. Then, as Chairman Minow and I had both expected, the political uproar began.

Affected VHF station operators climbed all over their members of Congress in protest. One such was the Travelers Insurance Company, which by now held the permit for Channel 3 in Hartford; another was the late August C. Meyer, a lawyer and banker of Champaign, Illinois, who held a similar permit in his hometown; and there were many others. The House Committee on Interstate and Foreign Commerce ordered hearings on the FCC's request for an All-Channel Receiver Law, which almost immediately evolved into a spirited fracas about de-intermixture.

(Several years later, when times had changed and a new set of "enemies" was on the horizon, I served on the board of MST, along with Augie Meyer. At every quarterly meeting, Augie, a banker at heart, would berate me for having caused him such expense in defending his monopoly position. At each meeting the cost of my disservice to him was greater than before, until finally, the founding chairman of MST, Jack Harris, loudly and publicly reminded Augie, whom I rather liked, personally, that he was trying to charge me compound interest on a bill I was never going to pay and that he ought to wise up and write it off. It was time to move on.)

At the congressional hearings, in 1962, the Travelers Insurance Company even trotted out the Irish-born incumbent governor of Connecticut, John Noel Dempsey (1915–1989), who testified that in 1953 when he was "mayor of a city in northeastern Connecticut" (he couldn't bring himself to mention the city's name, though he had been mayor there for twelve years, perhaps because my name was next on the published witness list), the city had been extremely grateful for the extensive coverage afforded by WTIC-TV during the statewide flooding associated with a hurricane. It remained for me to point out the most remarkable fact that the station which had performed this notable public service had not even gone on the air until two years after the flood waters had receded, and that furthermore, most of the power lines in Connecticut were also down as a result of the hurricane, so no one in the city of Putnam could have watched the station, anyhow.

At the same House Committee hearing, one of a tag-team pair of members of the committee would ask a "have you stopped beating your wife" type of question of the various FCC commissioners who appeared as witnesses for their bill, and then, while the question was being dutifully answered by the likes of Rosel Hyde, Bob Lee, or Newton Minow, the questioner would disappear from the dais and go out a back door. By the time he returned, the other was framing his next nasty question, and then he, too, rose to exit the room. Suspicious that no members of Congress could be having such recurrent bladder problems and/or be so visibly uninterested in the answer to a question he had raised, I ducked out the door of the meeting room in time to see the well-connected and brilliant lawyer for MST, Ernest Jenness, a partner in the law and lobbying firm of Covington and Burling, out in the corridor, feeding one of the pair the next verbal brickbat. Having little to lose, and knowing Ernie from the TASO discussions, I decided to help out my newfound friends on the Commission and walked up to the conversation saying, "Ernie, would you care to introduce me to your friend?"

When the first day's worth of hearings was finally gaveled to a close, I looked out the window to see that a steady rain had set in; it would be difficult for me to get back to Andy Kauffman's apartment without a severe wetting. I got lucky again! Standing at the same doorway on Capitol Hill, awaiting the FCC's van, was the Commission's occasional chairman, Rosel Hyde, ever courtly, ever polite and ever generous. "Bill, it's pretty damp here this evening and you'll never get a taxi in this weather; can we give you a lift?"

Chairman Minow did more than agree with my suggestions — and then face the wrath of some licensees, as mouthed by the MST-inspired House Committee members. He took the cause of UHF to the National Press Club and showed up as an invited luncheon guest with a large illustrated map of the United States, on which the FCC's Table of Television Allocations (the 6th Report and Order) was shown in graphic form. The VHF allocations were illuminated in red and the far greater number of UHF in green, which showed very dramatically the possibility for local service all across the nation that his Commission was setting out to make good on.

13

Building the Broadcast
Industry — Kitty's Station

[WLP] As soon as the All-Channel Receiver Law was enacted in 1962, to be effective in April of 1964, we set out to see what business prospects might develop from this long-awaited and advantageous development for UHF. Our initial rule was simple: Any decent-sized market where there were only two VHF stations had very clear room for a third network affiliate. There were many such places, and we selected three as the most likely to pay off for our shareholders — Dayton, Ohio; Raleigh, North Carolina; and Toledo, Ohio; — and decided to attack them in that order.

There had been a station in Dayton, on Channel 22, WIFE-TV, which had gone on the air with the first blush of the "thaw" in television grants at about the same time as WWLP, but, sadly, had lasted less than six months. There was still a good transmitter building (off Soldiers' Home and West Carrollton Road) numerous acres of sometime farmland, a tower and a GE helical antenna identical to ours at WWLP. The coaxial line up the tower and every item of equipment had been removed to satisfy creditors. In the fall of 1962, John Fergie and I went to Dayton, where I climbed the 620-foot tower to clean a ratty-looking bird's nest out of the antenna input adapter and check the antenna itself; while John looked over the other remnants. Then we made an offer for the place, as is, which was immediately accepted. The FCC handled our transfer request promptly, and in the spring of 1963, WKEF (as in the maiden name of my lady, Kathryn Elizabeth Flynn) became the first post–All-Channel Receiver Law station to go on the air.

We drew a management cadre from our staff at WWLP — John Fergie, the engineer who had been running WRLP, our satellite station in southwestern New Hampshire, as manager; and George Mitchell, who

178

Producer/director George Joseph Mitchell at Master Control.

had been Kitty's producer/director, as program director and back-up CEO. I always preferred to promote the devils I knew, from within, and I carry a couple of emotional scars to remind me of each time I have failed to follow this practice.

We knew that our competition was likely to make our life difficult; in fact, the Crosley station on Channel 2 and the Cox station on Channel 7 in Dayton managed to continue to hog all the good prime-time shows from all three networks. Two interesting conditions pertained. Apparently the networks were still willing to pay a premium in compensation to get a delayed or second-rate position for their programs on the V's, rather than take a very available live clearance on our station; and they insisted on giving the VHF station programmers the routine privilege of guessing wrong at the start of each new season and still being able to reclaim any subsequently more attractive network program from us on four weeks' notice. It was harsh, cruel and short-sighted, but it was just the way things were.

We quickly determined that CBS was well out of our reach, and not worth much effort. NBC, despite the good relations I enjoyed in

Springfield, was obviously happy with a ¾-time life on the Crosley station and had two other affiliations with it nearby, in Cincinnati and Columbus. ABC was the obvious target; we could offer complete, live and enthusiastic clearance on our "second-rate" frequency of 518–524 Mhz. Though this disability was very real at the outset, we knew that with every purchase of a new television receiver we were gaining in respectability. WKEF developed strong local programming aimed at kids, knowing they would teach their parents how to tune us in. Our friends at Massachusetts Mutual Life Insurance Company advanced us three million dollars to rebuild the station, and we drew on the profits of WWLP to support this nearly identical (facility-wise) sister station. Every few weeks, someone from the top management of Springfield Television — Ferguson, Filiault, Kitty or myself — would spend a day or two in Dayton. Very slowly, we climbed up to a respectable third position in the local Nielsen and ARB rating books.

After a few months, one of the WKEF engineers became bored at simply running the station's late evening movie and began a part-time switch to talent. He developed a character he called Dr. Creep, who introduced and promoted the late night movie by appearing from inside a casket, with appropriate sound effects. Soon Dr. Creep became so popular locally that the station had to buy him a special beard and clothing for his public appearances around the area.

Taxing Credulity

After WKEF had been on the air for several years, a group of local citizens organized themselves as Kittyhawk Television and filed to build a station (WKTR) on Channel 16, which was also available in the area. Soon they announced that they were going to seek a permanent affiliation with ABC, though we had by now become the de facto outlet for that network, attending their affiliates' meetings and even having been supplied with a huge plastic "meatball" to affix to the station's outer wall. We kept talking with the ABC people — Carmine Patti, the manager of affiliate relations, and his newly assigned local deputy, a sleazebag-in-waiting named Thomas G. Sullivan, who had replaced the regional manager, Bert

Julian, who had favored a firmer relationship with WKEF. After the other people were on the air, we began to sense a definite cooling in ABC's messages to us, though for some weeks, nothing outward occurred.

Then, in early November of 1969, the first shoe dropped: ABC officially announced they would entertain presentations for a fully-fledged, permanent affiliation to begin the following January, and invited applications. So, on the appointed day, all of us went to New York, hired a hotel room near the ABC headquarters and delivered our best pitch. Patti and those with him (which did not include Julian) did everything but yawn while we were demonstrating our virtues, most of which were facts already known to them, and left as quickly as they could without asking any follow-up questions. It was not a good sign, and we knew we were in deep trouble.

The announcement of our four-week cancellation notice came swiftly and as no shock. But George Mitchell, Berl Golub (WKEF's program director), and Wallace J. "Buzz" Sawyer (our corporate vice-president for programs), were up to the challenge, and soon acquired the rights to a lot of syndicated shows. We would soldier on! We also knew in our hearts that there was something very rotten about this whole fiasco; despite all its obfuscatory explanations, the network was leaving a well-equipped station with which it already had a viable relationship, that was run by experienced broadcasters with strong, respectable local programs, and that had a far better signal over the Dayton area — its decision didn't make sense. We smelled a large rat, maybe worse, and I asked our in-house counsel, Martin Edward Firestone, to exercise his legal ingenuity and find some way to drag the other station and ABC into a court of law where we could sort out the situation on the record.

We took our case for an injunction to the nearest Federal judge, the Hon. Timothy Sylvester Hogan (1909–1989) in Cincinnati. He read our presentation and the counter pleadings by the other parties, and said that the arguments given and the "statement of facts" by ABC had severely "taxed his credulity." Nevertheless, he refused our request for an injunction, stating that if we prevailed at trial, monetary damages would suffice to make us whole. So, on the first day of 1970, the ABC network went "across the street," we took down the meatball, and our lawsuit moved on to the deposition stage.

While Martin was doing his thing, Mitchell's new programs began doing theirs. WKEF stayed in a respectable third place during the midwinter

(February) Nielsen "sweep," seventh among all independents in the country, and ABC's new affiliate was a dismal fourth in Dayton. This was heartening and showed again that ABC had, indeed, made an inexplicable, and obviously stupid, decision. But, though heartening, that was nothing like what occurred after the close of the first day of depositions in Martin's lawsuit, in which he had been joined by partners from a prestigious firm that we hired to add impact to our complaint. We soon learned that after the testimony had been taken and the opposition parties had collectively adjourned to a local watering hole to celebrate our upcoming collapse, one principal of the other station, a Montgomery County (Ohio) elected judge named Craig Wright (which was a good name in Dayton, though we quickly dubbed him, "Judge Wrong"), mentioned to Jim Kelly, ABC's counsel, that if the other celebrators knew what he knew, they might not be quite so joyful.

Kelly was nobody's fool, and our engagement of other than in-house counsel showed that we were not likely to go quietly away in defeat, particularly if there were some dark, nefarious secrets that might soon come out. Kelly pumped Judge Wright/Wrong, and soon garnered enough information that he began to change sides in the further depositions — it would be far better for his client if ABC uncovered and cleaned up any unsavory behavior on its corporate part, than if we did it to and for them — they had a number of very valuable licenses (such as that Channel 7 in New York) that might be in jeopardy if this litigation were carried too far and a lot of bad behavior became exposed as a result of our pursuit. So, while ABC maintained a firm outward demeanor of calm, the depositions continued, though moved to the grander venues of New York and Washington. Meantime, legal discoveries continued and we began to accumulate quantities of evidence that there had been massive bribery at two levels of ABC — at the highest management levels, and at the Affiliations Department level, where we had felt that Carmine Patti, the second-in-command, was a major element in this fiasco.

During one of the follow-up depositions in New York, we were interrogating an influence-peddler named Joseph McMahon who had been hired by the Kittyhawk Television people to pass around some financial incentives to help them get the affiliation. His name having been mentioned in other depositions, he obviously knew who had received what, and for which, so our counsel had asked him to bring his records on the Kittyhawk matter.

"It was all oral, except for a few notes."

"You received a sub poena, *duces tecum*, did you not?"

"Yes, sir, but I could not find those notes. There is nothing in my office."

"Well, who might know of them, if you don't have them?"

"My former secretary, Mrs_____, but she has gone."

"And where is that lady now?"

"I have no idea. She gave us no forwarding address. Just quit and moved out of state, somewhere."

This was too obviously an attempt to hide the facts from our scrutiny, and as it was close to time for a luncheon break, we excused McMahon, who was planning to return across town to his office. I knew it would take him at least ten minutes, so I quickly called his office.

"Is Mrs_____ there?"

"No, she left us a few weeks ago."

"Damme! This is her cousin Bill, and I was hoping to have dinner with her while I'm here in New York. Do you know where she's gone to?"

"Yes, sir, she's in Florida."

Long before McMahon returned to his den, I had her current address, phone number, her hairdresser husband's new employer and much of the data that McMahon had been so outwardly unable to recall in deposition. That afternoon, the deposition continued. When confronted with the fact that we now had blown his dissembling alibi to bits, his memory returned, remarkably "refreshed" in the afternoon session. Among the tidbits we uncovered in this deposition was a copy of an invoice from a Dayton jewelry store, dated a week prior to the network switch announcement, for a bunch of watches engraved with the Kittyhawk station's call letters and the ABC network logo. The WKTR people had obviously felt that sufficient "fix" was in.

On another occasion, this time in Washington, Judge "Wrong," a devout pipe-smoker (who must have burned nearly as much in matches as in tobacco, for he was always relighting his pipe), was interrogating me. He was not enjoying the answers he was getting, for by this time, it was clear that we had instigated an increasing cascade of daylight into some highly questionable business practices and both parties of the opposition were verging onto the ropes. It would be Kelly's turn at me, again, the next morning, and we were all looking forward to see if his line of questioning was going to turn in our favor as much as we anticipated.

As we were gathering our papers at the end of the afternoon, I had found in my jacket pocket a book of those trick matches that are sold in joke shops, the kind that won't go out, and left them at my place on the table, next to my pen and note pad, when our team went off to regroup and have dinner with Andy Kauffman.

The next morning, Kelly's first question on the record, after I was sworn to tell the truth, the whole truth, etc., was: "Mr. Putnam, did you leave a book of trick matches on the table when you left here, yesterday?"

"Yes, sir. I left them at my place, but I can't find them here now."

Snickers broke out all around, and soon our team began to roar with laughter at the thought of Judge Wrong stealing my matches and then doing battle with them, maybe setting himself on fire.

◆ ◆ ◆

The Great Clean-up

In the end, all the litigation went away. On February 26, 1970, ABC officially announced it was terminating its current "contested" affiliation in Dayton and would seek a new presentation, and Jim Kelly asked me if we would return to make it. I had the great pleasure of telling him that we would never go back to talk with the kind of venal people we had been dealing with before. I made it very clear to Kelly that though we were not of a mind to be "bomb throwers" within the industry, we would carry this litigation on forever rather than have to do business with such people again, and that we fully expected to be treated decently by ABC, not made further game of. Soon thereafter, most of those we heartily distrusted either resigned or were fired, along with a number of other persons we had not yet come across reason to distrust.

We — and I remain sure that Kelly knew at least as much as we did, probably a lot more — had determined that ABC's man, Sullivan, who had been assigned the Dayton area just before we were dismissed, had previously been the executive of the Missouri Broadcasters Association, and had resigned that job after being caught embezzling the association's funds. In the Dayton situation, he was up to another old trick and had used a bogus name, John L. P. Daley, as a straw to whom WKTR's $20,000 "influence" checks were to be made out. We had uncovered redundant evidence that more loose cash had been ponied up by the Kittyhawk Television people and passed around ABC's Affiliations Department to help the network's people make a bad decision. We also knew, from reading the trade press, that certain top executives at ABC (the head of their owned and operated stations, Theodore H. Shaker, among others, though not the top man, Leonard Goldenson) had unexpectedly "taken early retirement" after another deposition uncovered evidence that some of the Kittyhawk corporate stock had been optioned to them.

In due course, more because we had come to like and trust Jim Kelly than any more sensible reason, we returned to that hotel room across 54th Street in New York and met with a wholly different reaction, and none of the same people; in fact, there was no one across the street on the 34th floor at ABC headquarters who had been there before. Everyone — all the district managers (people in the same category and managerial level as Paul Rittenhouse), all the receptionist/secretaries, Carmine Patti, whom we felt to have been a very key worm in the apple — all gone, even the one clean, good guy, Julian — all we gone except for the gravel-voiced and recently appointed vice-president, Richard L. Beesemeyer, whom we also believed to have been clean. It had been an exciting few months, as I telegraphed to my father, who was vacationing in Greece.

We could see little to gain by humiliating anyone in carrying the litigation forward, and we were offered a fair enough (though not overly generous) compensation rate from ABC and told to deal directly with Beesemeyer thereafter on any matters of concern. The Channel 16 Kittyhawk people gave their station and all its equipment to a local educational cooperative, run by one George Biersack, of the University of Dayton, whom we also rather liked. We didn't think about damages that we might collect from the local party that had so improperly offended us — they now had sufficient troubles as it was. Nor did we see any benefit to be gained in demanding something further from ABC. Securing a decent affiliation contract and compensation rate was reward enough, and besides, everyone who read the Dayton newspapers, or the broadcasting industry trade press, knew who had behaved poorly and how, as well as who had won that fight, why, and how.

One day, a few years later, "Beese" phoned me in Springfield to alert me (before I read it in the trade press) that ABC was in the process of signing an exclusive affiliation agreement with the new owners of Channel 2 — Crosley/Avco having sold out of the business. By now, I was a member of the NBC-TV Affiliates Board, and its secretary/treasurer; I wouldn't mind in the least having to do business with the people at 30 Rock for two stations rather than just one, and I guess Dick Beesemeyer knew it. After a bit of dickering we began a relationship with Tony Cervini and Don Mercer at NBC, and WKEF left ABC quietly — but found its way back there some years after we had sold our stations.

◆   ◆   ◆

An Adventure in Raleigh

As soon as we had begun to successfully digest the investment we had made in Dayton, we assayed the waters elsewhere, and made an application for another Channel 22 which was also allocated in Raleigh, North Carolina. Here there was a similar network clearance situation, but this time with NBC being the odd network out, for ABC was paying handsomely to get full clearance on Channel 5, WRAL-TV, the station on which the future five-term, reactionary and self-styled "red neck" senator, Jesse Alexander Helms (1921–2004), then delivered editorials.

Somewhat to our chagrin, a local group, headed by the former governor and senator James Terry Sanford, also made an application for the same channel. We sized them up, and decided that half a loaf, shared with the likes of the admirable and idealistic Mr. Sanford (1917–1998), would be satisfactory, and offered to merge, 50/50, half their money and half ours, with us to furnish the know-how and industry contacts, and with Governor Sanford joining our Board of Directors.

We very much respected him and he came north to attend a Springfield Television Board meeting on Asnebumskit Hill, after which several of us were to drive to New York and discuss an affiliation while having dinner with NBC's then vice-president for affiliations, the late Thomas E. Knode. This turned out to not be the pleasant gathering I had hoped for. When we arrived at the appointed restaurant, Tom had obviously been swilling a few while awaiting us; he was belligerent, cursing repeatedly while muttering about never wanting to affiliate with another UHF station. Tom was visibly unimpressed with Governor Sanford and continued to order drinks, while the rest of us ordered food.

As the evening wore on, Tom spent most of his time cursing anything that came to mind, while continuing to imbibe. In due course, he actually slid under the table, cursing all the while, until he lay flat on the terrazzo floor. John Fergie, Rollie Jacobs and I extricated him and propped him into a taxi headed for an address we found in his wallet. I never saw Tom again. NBC soon dispensed with his services and we soldiered on in Raleigh, sending Jacobs, one of our most congenial employees, to be the manager at the putative WJHF.

Though we went through all the, by now, usual planning and had even sent the genial Rollie from his on-the-air job in Springfield to take up residence in Raleigh, things were not going well, we sensed, with our partnership. This became particularly evident in the matter of purchasing a tower. I had received a call from one of the officers at Capitol Cities Broadcasting, asking if I'd be interested in purchasing a used tower, 1,200 feet of it, for which they had no further use; it had been taken down and was stacked on the ground near Albany. I knew these to be honest folk and the price of $150,000 seemed right, so I called for a concurrence on

The genial Rollie Jacobs took over the Sports Desk when Burleigh Brown went to WRLP.

the part of our southern partners — and the tower was soon on its way south, on the back of several flatbed trucks. We told the teamsters to unload the tower on the ground at the site we had determined for our transmitter and we then asked Sanford's finance man, Bill White, to repay Springfield Television for its half of the purchase price.

Soon I received a cashier's check for $75,000 from a bank in Raleigh along with a copy of a mortgage note made out to the bank, pledging the tower — my whole tower — as security for Bill White's loan. When I called White to express my dismay with his actions, he told me that all I had to do was mortgage "the other half" of my tower and I'd be whole. This smelled like a primrose financial path that I had a great fear of going down, and Springfield's Board of Directors soon decided this arrangement wasn't going to work, so both parties would be smart to divorce while we were still on speaking terms. Sanford knew that we had been out of pocket for several other expenses, like Rollie's relocation, and arranged for the sale of our construction permit for $50,000, with the earnest money coming into our treasury. When that sale fell through, we kept the money, and Sanford then arranged a second sale for another $50,000 of earnest money, which also fell apart.

Rollie packed up again and prepared to return home. The mortgage was discharged and the tower was reloaded and sent off to the Guzewicz factory for a derustification and renewal process called "wheelabrating," and thence to Dayton, where it gave us the tallest tower in the area and kept Ray Mercier's successor busy for a couple of weeks.

Some years later the Channel 22 station in Raleigh was actually built, and it did become an NBC-TV affiliate.

A Good Deed in Toledo

When we set out to explore the construction of a station in Toledo, where there were also two VHF stations and a Channel 24 allocation, John Fergie and I made plans to go to that city and look the place over. In the meantime, a local warehousing entrepreneur named Daniel Harrison Overmyer announced that he was going to apply for the same channel. He also announced that he was going to be opening stations in numerous other markets and, for a very brief interval, some of the more gullible in the trade press of broadcasting even published stories about "the Overmyer Network" and its pioneering genius, though there was not one tangible item of broadcasting to be found. Martin Firestone soon advised us that we would be heading for a comparative hearing, where the local entity, Overmyer, unless actually a convicted criminal, would have a great leg up over any out-of-towners, particularly a multiple owner like Springfield Television had become. Meantime, we found a real estate agent who pointed us at some land east across the Maumee River for a transmitter site which John, our corporate engineer at the time, went over to look at, while I asked the real estate man if he knew anyone that could give me some lowdown on Overmyer — information that might be helpful to us in case of a comparative hearing.

I was directed to the office of a small-time lawyer who had represented Overmyer's mother and a local bank when Daniel had sued to have her declared incompetent and the bank collusive with her in withholding his share of his father's estate. The trial had become quite nasty, in the midst of which Overmyer had obtained control of a local weekly newspaper and proceeded to pillory the poor lawyer so mercilessly that he had been forced into personal bankruptcy. I located him in a walk-up garret office.

In due course, and despite all the unsavory acts that the lawyer soon recounted to me, Martin Firestone argued convincingly that we would lose in a comparative hearing — even against such a questionable character as we now knew Overmyer to be, so we opted to withdraw our application, with Overmyer compensating us for any out-of-pocket expenses. I contacted the lawyer and told him that we were not going ahead, but that he should send me a bill for his consulting services to date. He promptly sent me a bill for a paltry $50, for the hour's worth of conversation. I called him back, saying this sum could not be nearly correct, and suggested that since Overmyer was going to pay the bill, he should move the decimal point over a bit. So, he did — two places — and I felt like a Boy Scout.

There was a bit of a sequel. I had also written to various building commissions in the cities where Overmyer had told the FCC that he owned warehouses, so as to prove his solvency and ability to construct a station as applied for. In due course the letters were answered; in some cities there was actually a building (though not always owned by Overmyer), but in most of them, there was not even a building permit issued for a vacant lot. Overmyer's balance sheet — as submitted to the

FCC — was largely a fiction, and a bank on Long Island was also offering to lend him many millions of dollars on the strength of these nonexistent warehouses. A couple of years later, I was not surprised to learn that the bank, too, had collapsed because of its multitude of bad loans. Federal overseers saw that every tangible asset tumbled into the vaults of the First National Bank of Boston (and thence into the momentarily tottering, but handsomely overpaid, hands of the Bank of America). Moreover, by the end of the next decade Overmyer had been convicted of bankruptcy fraud and the entire Toledo warehousing operation had collapsed.

So much for overly creative accounting.

A Yankee Lawyer

Among the second tier of potential station locations that we considered was Charlotte, North Carolina. There were three operating stations already on the air, but one of them was owned by Cy Nesbe Bahakel (1919–2006), a local politician and UHF-TV operator whom we felt to be vulnerable to the loss of his ABC network affiliation in the face of a well-managed broadcasting firm like Springfield Television. We began to make preparations for filing an application, among the first of which was securing a site for our transmitter; so I thought about who might be available to go make a deal with some farmer on the north side of town for an option to build on his land.

Of all our management personnel, Martin Firestone, who had previously been on the staff of the FCC, was based in Washington and so was nearest to Charlotte. So I told him to fly down there and scout out the situation — but be sure to come home with a credible transmitter site option agreement.

Several days went by with no word from Martin and I began to get antsy. Then, finally, after another day, he called in.

"What in hell have you been wandering around there doing?"

"Talking to farmers, Boss."

"Well, did you get an option? It shouldn't cost us too much."

"No option yet, Boss."

"Well, what in hell have you been doing?"

"Calm down, Boss! Calm down. You just have no idea how the farmers around here feel about a Jewish lawyer working for a Yankee company."

I told him to come home; a construction permit in Charlotte wasn't so attractive that we needed that fight on top of whatever else we might encounter.

◆ ◆ ◆

Competing with the Church

When the wars over the All-Channel Law were safely concluded, the late Jack Harris, one of the primest movers of the television broadcasting industry, and long-time manager of the *Houston Post*'s KPRC-TV, asked if I would now care to join the board of the Maximum Service Telecasters, the "enemy" group that I had finally been instrumental in defeating. I saw this invitation as a good way to influence lots of things in a manner favorable to Springfield Television, so I accepted. I very much respected Jack, and remain certain that he was subsequently influential in pushing my election as vice-chairman of MST and to the NBC-TV Affiliates Board, as well as in behind-the-scenes support of Kitty's candidacy for the NAB-TV Board.

At one subsequent MST board meeting, in Palm Springs, the topic turned to various proposals then being made to the FCC for abbreviating the standard mileage separations, so as to shoehorn VHF stations into various markets without adhering to all the regulatory mileage protections that the FCC engineering rules called for. One of the markets where this "drop-in" idea had been proposed was Salt Lake City. I saw the idea of a short-spaced Channel 13 as a threat to UHF service generally, while most of the others on the MST Board saw these proposals as incipient threats to the sanctity of their own coverage areas. When our formal meeting drew to a close, the current chairman, Arch L. Madsen, president of the LDS Church's broadcasting arm, Bonneville International, proprietors of KSL-TV in Salt Lake City and KIRO-TV in Seattle, announced — to amazed applause — that he would be hosting a cocktail party at 6 P.M. that evening.

During his soiree, I cornered the host in a quiet moment and suggested: "Maybe I should go into competition with you in Salt Lake, Arch; there's a Channel 20 available."

"That's a risky idea, Bill; but if you decide to do it, we'll find you a good transmitter location, and then I'll introduce you around town."

"Let me think about it a bit, Arch, and get back to you. I can't afford to run a charity for the industry, so the investment has got to be able to pay its way. But I think the All-Channel Law is as far advanced in Salt Lake as anywhere in the country. Channel 20 would be as good a prospect in the long run, I think, as any short-spaced Channel 13. Would you also consider running a few PSAs telling people how to tune to Channel 20? We can tape 'em for you in Springfield."

"Not only will we run some on KSL-TV, Bill, but I'll get the other V's in town to do so, as well."

Arch was as good as his word, and we soon built KSTU.

A year or so later, after we had built the station, as the only independent in town, we had to counter-program the network affiliates, particularly their ten o'clock news segments. We did this by scheduling the ribald and irreverent British export, *Bennie Hill*, in that time period. Then, one day, a well-known local agitator against "bad" television programming called up our station manager, Bill Pepin, to warn him that she would be organizing a public protest about the airing of *Bennie Hill* unless KSTU cancelled it right away. Sensing a good promotional opportunity, Pepin consulted briefly with his advisors at WWLP and then called the lady back to ask if it would be okay if he told the newspapers and the other TV stations in town about this protest demonstration, so she could get the maximum publicity for the event.

Andy Kauffman had a relative in Salt Lake City, a well-traveled mining engineer named Arthur Zeldin, with whom Kitty and I had dinner one night, at his home on the fringe of one of the golf courses on the city's fashionable "Benches" area. While the ladies were preparing dinner, Arthur and I had been discussing the business climate of the quasi-religious city-state that Deseret had become, noting *inter alia* that it appeared to me to be "the last bastion of the Yankee work ethic."

"You may be right, Bill," replied Arthur, "but you should know that I've traveled all over the world working for Kennecott Mining, and everywhere they've sent me, I've been a Jew. Until, that is, I was recalled to the home office here in Salt Lake, and now I find that I'm a Gentile."

◆   ◆   ◆

We explored the possibilities of constructing stations in several other communities. Morrill Ring and I flew out to consider transmitter sites in Kansas City—and interview Harry Truman. I went alone to look over the terrain near Austin. Fergie, Kitty and I even spent a couple of days probing the environment in Jacksonville, and Erica and Lowell were dispatched to snoop and interview folk in the vicinity of Spokane, which last was personally attractive to me because of that market's existing stations' large, though unsalable, circulation in southwest Canada; but these probes were all discontinued when we received an offer to buy the entire Springfield Television Corporation. However, in due course, after Springfield Television had become history, these other putative UHF stations were all built and operated profitably.

14

Glimpsing the Future

[KBP] In the winter of 1983 a group of professors from MIT came to visit Bill on the mountain and wanted to talk about the future of astronomical research. A few weeks later another bunch of professorial types arrived from Princeton to continue our education on the future of astronomical research. They particularly wanted to impress on value of a proposal that was then pending before NASA for the placement of a telescope in orbit high above the Earth's atmosphere. We were flattered by all this exalted academic attention, but really didn't grasp why we were the object of it.

Then, one day, the phone rang and it was George Wallerstein, a fellow member of the American Alpine Club, and professor of astronomy at the University of Washington. He had been a pen pal of Bill's for a number of years, as Bill's was the general editor of the Club's guidebooks to the mountains of Western Canada, where George had done quite a bit of exploratory alpinism in the Monashee Range. At last, Bill could ask a frank question about this most unusual, high-class astronomical attention of someone who we knew would tell us the unvarnished truth.

"George, what's with all these bigshot professors from MIT and Princeton who've been calling on us here about some telescope in Space? Apparently it's supposed to be even greater than sliced bread. But my little brother, Michael, is the trustee of Lowell Observatory. You guys should be talking with him — not me. He's chairman of classics at Brown University in Providence."

"That's fine, but Bill, it's *your* attention we want. You're the guy who can get this idea jarred loose from the Congress and into action."

"How'm I supposed to do that?"

"Your congressman, Edward Boland, is chairman of the appropriations subcommittee that has jurisdiction over NASA, and he's opposed to the idea of a space telescope."

"So, who told on me? You guys want me to speak with Eddie for you."

"You're not so slow, Bill, after all."

"All right! For you, George, I'll look into it."

We promptly called my son, Morgan, who was then the administrative aide to Mr. Boland, and determined, in conversation, that the congressman's reluctance was merely financial. Was this massive new item going to be cost effective? He did not have anything against the advancement of astronomy.

On his next visit home, Bill had a few words with the late Mr. Boland, and the deed was soon done. However, with the benefit of hindsight, he should have seen to it, while he had the chance, to get the space telescope named for the true discoverer of the expansion of the universe, the somewhat reclusive successor director of his great-uncle Percival Lowell's observatory, Vesto Melvin Slipher, rather than Edwin Hubble, the man who probed deeply into Slipher's knowledge and then published the most papers on the topic, a dozen years after V. M. Slipher's pioneering work on identifying the "red shift" in the spectrum of the Andromeda Nebula.

A few years later, when Michael had to be out of the country for an extended period, he turned over the sole trusteeship of the observatory to Bill, who promptly got even with George by drafting him to serve as chairman of a search committee to recommend a new director for Lowell Observatory.

◆ ◆ ◆

Good Night, My Love

By the spring of 1983, we had been in the television business for more than 30 years and had achieved substantial ego gratification, prosperity for our shareholders, and a reasonable measure of personal security. Both of

Newsman Morgan Broman, of the second generation, later administrative aide to Congressman Edward Boland.

us were contemplating some sort of successorship, so we asked our children, Bill's son, Lowell, and my daughter, Erica, to step up and take part in some of our duties. Lowell thus did an occasional on-the-air editorial, while Erica, only two years younger than he, worked in the newsroom and also stood in admirably for me on *At Home with Kitty*, rather than having the station laboriously tape hour-long programs for my occasional absences. Bill had served a prominent stint on the NBC TV Affiliates Board and was vice-chairman of MST; I had been chairman of the NAB TV Board and was president of the Television Information Office (but it was Bill alone who was inducted into the Broadcasting Hall of Fame in 2001). However, Lowell was far more interested in computerizing our traffic operation. He designed his own business system, which we came to install, and which became the foundation of his subsequent enterprise, Video Communications, Inc (VCI). Erica continued for some time as talent on WATR-TV and is still a personality on what Bill calls "begathons" for the local PBS station in Springfield, WGBY.

The building of our stations and status had been challenging and mostly fun, but nothing could go on forever, and frank conversations with our children determined that running TV stations was not on their dream list, so we allowed to ourselves that we'd consider selling "our" stations. After all, the shareholders had not been receiving vast dividends, and we sensed that most were patiently holding out for an ultimate reward in the form of large capital gains. Furthermore, and what was more important, the business of television broadcasting had now become "mature"— more the domain of bean counters than builders, of pragmatists than programming idealists. Complicating, but reinforcing, our thinking was the fact that the Federal Communications Commission was now clearly embarking hellbent on a policy of "marketplace regulation"— poor taste, inaccurate and misleading news reporting, and ever more salacious language were increasingly frequent on the nation's airwaves. Bob Lee was long retired, and no one even mentioned the morality of management or the national origin of licensee ownership any more; overlapping or multiple ownership restrictions were rapidly becoming a thing of the past. There was no further interest in protecting the concept of "the public interest," however loosely and inconsistently it was applied; what the public was willing to patronize was what the public airwaves should carry. This was all a far cry from the television we had grown up with, and we did not like its evolution.

Our executive vice-president, the now late Paul Alphonse Brissette (1931–2010), successor to the retired Jim Ferguson, who had broached the delicate question of a sale, began sounding out potential buyers, and we, who had other activities to demand our concentration, naively trusted him to act in the shareholders' best interest. Though the ultimate price we received was quite reasonable — particularly so after the two of us took the buyer, Stephen Adams, to court to obtain redress for some of his misleading statements and broken promises (which we later learned had been engineered by Brissette). Neither to Bill nor myself was it disclosed that Brissette had been mostly concerned with making a secret deal with the buyer that benefitted him, rather

Another of the second generation, W. Lowell Putnam, later the founder of Video Communications, Inc.

than upholding his legal duty — to protect the shareholders for whom he was supposedly working. In a subsequent deposition, Adams was forced to admit that he and Brissette had knowingly misled us about many things, and that he knew that if he had told us the truth about his intentions regarding the stations we had built and the employees we had come to love and care for, we would never have agreed to a sale (which Bill, personally, had the votes to block in the ensuing, legally required, shareholders' meeting).

In the painful, expensive and brutal litigation that followed the sale, which the two of us initiated to force Adams to live up to his handshake promises regarding ourselves, we learned a number of unsavory details about the role of Brissette in the sale, information which was compounded by the unethical conduct of the lawyers they hired to defend themselves. This was all further confused by a very cosy relationship between Adams and his loan officer at CIGNA, whose private notes ultimately gave away all the dirty details, forcing Adams to pony up seven figures' worth of additional cash in a settlement.

Be all that as it was, the television industry has now changed so much that we are happily out of it, and the shareholders of Springfield Television received — for the opportunity their investment had enabled, the jobs we had been given, and the hard work, long days, sleepless nights, and abusive depositions that Bill, Ercia and I subsequently endured — a return on their original investment (which varied from $10 initially in 1952, up to $15 per share in 1954 and 1962) of more than 3,000 percent.

15

Personalities

[WLP] Since these are personal recollections, the views expressed in this penultimate section are solely those of this writer (definitely not those of his less-opinionated wife), and are herein unaffected by whatever may remain from the late Fairness Doctrine. As well, they reflect (as the two of us prepare for our entry into the unknown hereafter) not one iota of anything else. Furthermore, the FCC is now composed of five members, back to its original (1934) complement, and we note that those who favored increased competition have generally been those appointed by Democratic presidents.

In retrospect it is interesting to observe that of the members of the Federal Communications Commission whom I remember most clearly, quite a few stand out as "good guys." I rank them below, in my personal order of their intellectually honest adherence to the public interest:

1. Bob Lee, a Chicago Republican and a very good guy, needs no further comment from either of us. We loved him, and he became our good friend, even visiting us in Flagstaff after we had all retired from the fray of broadcasting. Though gone, now, for 20 years, we miss him to this day, and recall his fondness for advising complainers about the FCC to be grateful they didn't get all the government they were paying for.

2. Frieda Barkin Hennock (1904–1960), a Ukrainian-born New York academic, was the first woman appointed to the FCC (by Harry Truman). She cared enough to listen to the woes of UHF broadcasters, for she had been party to the decision to open up that band to television, but she was replaced as soon as Mr. Truman left office.

3. Newton Norman Minow (eighty-four years of age, at this writing), though unpopular with many telecasters, still swarms with integrity, which he has passed on to his children. He must have read St. Paul's second epistle to the Corinthians, where in Chapter 3 (v. 6) one can learn

that *the spirit of the law quickeneth, whereas the letter often killeth.* Anyhow, he was helpfully devoted to the spirit of the Communications Act of 1934.

4. Kenneth A. Cox (b. 1916), a bureaucratic, but very idealistic, protégé of Washington's late Senator Warren Grant Magnusson, had been chief of the Broadcast Bureau and had his ear to the ground of broadcasting. Broadcasters always knew where they were at with him.

5. Rosel H. Hyde (1900–1972), a Republican from Utah, was invariably kind, sympathetically polite and gentlemanly. I considered him a friend.

6. James Henry Quello (1914–2010) (Happy), a former broadcaster, understood the game and was always willing to listen attentively.

7. Emil William Henry (1928–), a Yale-educated lawyer from Tennessee, was the one who asked that critically important, for us, anyway — but legally irrelevant — question about Triangle Publications.

8. Abbott McConnell Washburn (1915–2003) (Doc), a university professor and sometime maritime administrator, was studious and tried

Up, up and away — our third tower (1980) on Provin Mountain. Note the 9-inch coaxial line.

to be polite and informed. On one office visit, when I urged that he take the lead in a momentarily controversial matter, he replied, "Bill, there's an old Danish proverb that goes: *'there is no profit in stirring a turd.'*"

9. Robert T. Bartley (1910–1988) (Bashful), Speaker Sam Rayburn's nephew, was polite but uninterested — discouraged "by FCC practices."

10. Lee Loevinger (1913–2004), a semi-pro bureaucrat, had been head of the Antitrust Division at the Department of Justice. In that capacity, before he was "elevated" to the FCC, I made an appointment and asked him to look into the proposed acquisition by Varian Brothers of the Eitel/McCullough Company, the only two makers of final power amplifier tubes for UHF-TV in the United States. I pointed out that this merger, if allowed, would have the unintended result of stifling development of klystrons, to the ongoing detriment of UHF television. He was uninterested. Thereafter, we sought to purchase such tubes from EEV — English Electric Valve — and a number of other stations followed our example.

The mountain, as we left it in 1984, with our second and third towers.

11. Dean Burch (1927–1991), a Nixon appointee from Arizona, came to the FCC pre-programmed, already knew everything he needed, and didn't care to learn more.

13. George McConnaughey (1897–1966), an Eisenhower appointee and former attorney for Ohio Bell, cared mostly for limiting competition and didn't converse with me.

After Bob Lee retired, I started to become discouraged by the turn of regulation that the FCC was taking — toward what a later chairman called "a marketplace approach." To some, this apparently meant the end of unrealistic fumbling with what constituted that belabored term "public interest," but to others, it meant a relaxed, money-based approach to almost everything, a condition I was not sure Kitty and I were prepared to be happy with. This may have been somewhat inconsistent on my part; after all, I had done ferocious political and bureaucratic battle for UHF and my concept of the public interest, with the FCC staff, many of its members, much of the industry and quite a few members of Congress. But age was creeping up on the two of us; we had come reasonably close to winning all our fights and might even be able to consider ourselves respectably ahead of the game.

Any questions?

16

A Poetic Heritage Comes Out

[KBP] I'm told there have been some notable literary figures in his ancestry — Bill mentions his great-aunt Amy and grandmother, née Elizabeth Lowell, quite often — but I suspect that many of those people would have started rolling in their graves if they became aware of the poetic distortions that Bill frequently came up with. It often took him several weeks to draft and then finish composing a verse; he'd carry those drafts around, take them on long plane trips, and sleep on them often. After delivering them, he tended to forget these compositions, but I saved them all, a good many of which pertained to figures we knew in television.

Here's one that he composed and delivered in New York on April 24, 1979, at a dinner I helped organize for the NBC-TV Affiliates' Board in honor of the retirement of a man we deeply respected, NBC's executive vice-president, David C. Adams (1914–1999), who had once been on the staff of the FCC. Bill spoke for all the affiliates of NBC:

In years gone by, Dave, you and I, debated many things;
The ratings, rates, our loves and hates, and what tomorrow brings.
Of whirling discs, those prime-time risks, and ultra cable pie;
Of who's on first, and who's the worst, the "meatball" or the "eye."

But now the order changes and gone are days of yore,
Behold the distant ranges, begone the ancient lore.
The heralds of tomorrow are heard throughout the land,
But their message carries sorrow, and they need a guiding hand.

We understand your leaving, and with tears we let you go,
You leave us mostly grieving, for flowers 'neath the snow.
Though festive is the mood tonight, and joyful we all seem
We pray that things will go all right, when you're not on the team.

For though we've argued long and hard on how to run this show,
We know you're made of true blue stuff, the finest that we know.

You speak as one who knows us well, and we respond in kind,
With us you really ring the bell, when others seem so blind.

But now the order changes and gone are days of yore,
A new rank soon arranges, that plays a different score.
The trumpets of tomorrow are loud throughout the land,
Their sound may not bring sorrow, but they'll miss your guiding hand.

So we who've had the pleasure of working well with you,
Have one more task to measure — to bid the right adieu.
There's wine galore in every glass, there's pride in every eye,
To David — you've got plenty class — farewell, but not goodbye.

Here's another that he delivered only a month later, at the regular
NBC-TV Affiliates meeting in Los Angeles, in which he managed to work
in a lot of the NBC brass and all members of the Affiliates Board and
which he entitled "*The (Ancil) Payne of It All*:"

Tampa Bay is Faber's town, where football has a slim renown,
But Bill is brave and fights for fees, has Cory Dunham on his knees.
Krueger comes from Idaho, a place where elephants all go.
They die, but Bob he lives in style, winning ratings all the while.
Jackson comes from Louisville, and keeps our records in a still,
Ralph writes the minutes, mails the checks and keeps the network
    off our necks.

On old Great Muddy there he sits, KSD's Ray Karpowicz;
If Central Time zone gets the shaft, he'll put his outfit on a raft,
And float it down to Royal Street to see if Yager can be beat.
But Jim is seldom under par; we'll hitch our wagon to his star.
If Springfield seems a little duller, you simply haven't met Don Moeller.
His town's the same as mine, you see, which means that he's as good
    as me,
A thought my ego cannot brook and so I'll quickly turn and look...

To Mike McCormick, Beertown's best, a cut above the normal rest.
Fierce and tough, he's no spring lamb, a fitting heir to the great
    god Damm.
Now, if a trick or two you'd learn, head for Texas and Blake Byrne.
In Fort Worth and Dallas, too, he's number one or sometimes two.
Ruby's in the Great Southwest, where all the cactus wrens still nest.
He golfs and skis the whole year 'round and clears saguaros at a bound.

And finally now, our fearless leader, like his totem pole of cedar,
He, whose tireless sense of humor turns aside the evil rumor,

That soon we'll all enjoy less clover, for now his reign is nearly over.
Thus he joins the elder hams, as list that's headed by Hod Grams,
And Uncle Bob and Louis Read, and our industry's Sam Snead,
So maybe Jack will teach him how to run KING television, now.

At the Affiliates Board meeting held at Dorado Beach on Puerto
Rico, on the evening of November 26th, 1979, he delivered a timely trib-
ute, mostly to his predecessor as secretary/treasurer of the NBC Affiliates,
Ralph Jackson, CEO of WAVE-TV, the NBC-TV affiliate in Louisville.

The joy which we now show to you, is shared by almost all
Directors old and even new, the short ones and the tall,
The waiters and the network brass, 'most everyone you've met,
They think that you've got plenty class; On that you sure can bet.

Yet to this overriding glee there is a small deception
Dissent is heard from only me, I am the one exception.
For when you said, "Please take my job," You said I need not shirk.
You did not say I'd have to rob, nor tell me of the work.

You 'lowed that there was plenty dough and prospects sure were rosy,
You failed to say what I now know, I should have been more nosey.
The secretary parts a cinch — a letter or a verse —
Though now and then there is a pinch and I begin to curse.

That query into network ways — How much do we conspire?
Caused me to labor many days, and even to perspire.
For if we run them, that is bad, but if we don't it's worse;
Thank God our record keeping's sad and minutes all are terse.

As treasurer I have no joy, for you I have no love;
I should have seen that you were coy and said, "That part you shove."
The bills of which I did not know that cleaned us out of cash,
For trips on which I did not go and other things more rash,

I could not argue with you, though nor even call you back,
For once I had said, "Maybe so," you had a heart attack.
You've been around this mill, I know; the reason for this party;
You're well and have a healthy glow, indeed you're hale and hearty.

So I'll not dwell upon that sin, the work you dumped upon me;
Should I become your gracious twin, blessings would abound me.

On January 4, 1980, he wrote a poem for the retirement party of the late Robert Francis Donahue, a longtime fixture in local radio management, who came to work as station manager for WWLP after WMAS was sold:

For this event I had one job, to write a poem about our Bob,
And with my talents as a bard, that wasn't really very hard.
I wondered if I ought to tell about the days he used to sell
Space in papers and on the air, a stunt that takes a special flair.
But here with all this friendly mob, I would not dare to —
    insult our Bob.

And so I thought of long ago when he — and God — found radio;
When late at night, I'd try to get a far-off place on a crystal set.
With distant stations on the air from KHQ to Congress Square,
Though it was corn, still on the cob; 'twas when he started —
    our friend Bob.

A Minnesota boy at heart, he just came East to get a start;
Among the outlets that he knew were some in Boston, Lowell, too.
He stopped here only for a rest upon his way back to the West
And spend a while, perhaps hobnob with upper crust folk —
    just like Bob.

Some forty years ago, I guess, was when he started 'MAS.
And twenty years ago, I said, "Come work with us, we need your head."
We needed someone filled with couth to counteract our sometime youth.
We didn't need another slob; and that is why I —
    sought out Bob.

We needed someone filled with fact, who knew the score and had some tact,
To make a friend or make a speech, or amplify our station's reach.
We needed someone we could trust, with iron health, who'd never rust,
Who'd bring our audience a throb; we really needed —
    good old Bob.

But now you say it's time to go, to turn and look at what you know,
And make a place for someone who will never be as good as you.
For in your place will never fit a man of equal grace and wit.
With love, with pride and with a sob, we toast your health —
    a great man, Bob.

On the 16th of November, 1980, coincidentally Bill's mother's 88th birthday, he delivered this one to the NBC Affiliates' Board's fall meeting on Maui, at the request of his friend and incoming Affiliates' Board chairman,

Fred Paxton, late owner of the Paducah *Sun/Democrat* and the city's only television station. Paxton had asked Bill to produce a special greeting for NBC's new leader, Fred Silverman:

Said Chairman Fred, "Unless you're dead, you'd better have a verse
Or when we reach that island beach, I'll see you in a hearse."
Commands like this are hard to miss, and so I stirred my muse;
But if some word should sound absurd — please blame it on the booze.

I thought of when, three years ago, we met just down the way;
How many were the issues which divided us that day.
We did agree that NBC, a network — so we heard —
Both red and blue had lost their glue; its peacock was in turd.

The chimes were gone, the snake forlorn; Nebraska owned the N.
The Paul Klein show, with all its snow, was leading with a ten.
In vain we'd hunt another stunt, to hype a rating sweep;
But every try just went awry, and we could only weep.

Recall that day of disarray, when no one ran the show;
And Chairman Payne, with high disdain, displayed his chart of flow.
Aye, though with drink and festive glee, we tried to mask the fact,
Let's face it friends, old NBC was flat upon its back.

Affiliates were losing faith and clearances declining.
The peacock, aimless as a wraith, could find no cloud with lining.
Into this tomb of boundless gloom could reach no ray of hope.
Indeed, it seemed that we just simply couldn't cope.

Back then it seemed that we were creamed; non-profit was our status.
And sheriffs all across the land were making noises at us.
We'd only see un*Happy Days,* or aim a pox at *MASH*es.
Among three networks we were fourth; our peacock sat in ashes.

Into this scene so dank and mean, the web of "also ran;"
Came saving force — without a horse — our Hi Ho Silverman.
He leveled with us from the start; that step renewed our will.
His beefed up brass with plenty class will soon rebuild our till.

No words we mince, the guy's a prince; our faith in him is great.
(I say this 'cause we took a vote that came out five to eight.)
So, with a joy that does not cloy and trust that grows each day,
We toast his health, his life, his wealth; his spirit lights our way.

And as we gather once again on Maui's sandy shore
The peacock flies through clearing skies, new heights he seeks to soar.
This fine estate, we now relate, all jesting put aside;
It must be said is due to Fred; he gives us back our pride.

◆   ◆   ◆

Peter Hamar, who joined us after Bob Vadnais retired, brought with him a small backhoe/bucket loader that Bill enjoyed using. Pete also built us a more direct route up the mountain to the station and thus merited a farewell poem when he announced that he was retiring to Florida as of the 1st of March, 1981:

They said that I should write a verse about our Polish Prince
And how he holds up Provin Mount with baling wire and splints.
And so I thought of all he'd done with roofs and floors and halls,
But fortunately I still know just which are bearing walls.
That is a secret I shall hold, for all eternity,
For as you all can plainly see, it's job security.

Throughout the history of mankind, a few great names appear
Whose fame derives from having helped to get from there to here.
A Scotsman named MacAdam stands among the foremost rank;
'Twas he who broke the pristine rock upon the mountain flank,
And left his name in history books that others, too, might learn;
Just fill the road with rocks, my friends, so that the wheels won't churn.

And we've all heard of Hannibal, the enemy of Rome,
Who lost the war, but won great fame by bringing from his home
Great elephants from Africa, through Spain and then through France.
Across the glaciers of the Alps, he made those beasties prance.
A student of such feats as these is our guest here tonight,
When he sets out to build a road, he surely does it right.

Since elephants are out of style, and hard to come by, too,
He had the Downeys move the rocks, except the ones he blew.
And every standing tree in sight became a two by four.
The place looked like a battleground left over from some war.
But finally, it got sorted out, and grass commenced to grow;
The culverts, pipes and whatnot in, the waterfall to flow.

It's wide and straight, both up and down, as all of us attest.
It reaches from the gravel pit right to the very crest;
A tribute to his workmanship, his know-how and his skill.
In fact, his boots are going to be extremely hard to fill.
And so we reach our mountaintop by Hamar's fancy trail,
A landmark to our Polish Prince, a friend we're proud to hail.

The television industry's poet had a busy time in the late spring of 1981; there was his by-now-traditional poem [1] for the NBC Affiliates' meeting on May 18, and he was retiring from that board and as the Affiliates'

secretary/treasurer—a job he inherited from Ralph Jackson and passed on to Bill Faber. In early June, Don Mercer, vice-president for Affiliations at NBC retired [2]; and a week later our beloved chief engineer at WWLP, Don Shaw, died suddenly [3]. Another week after that sad event, Bill delivered the industry's farewell [4] to the Good Commissioner, our dear friend Bob Lee, at a special dinner which I helped arrange and we both attended in Washington:

I

I'll take one wistful moment now, before I take my final bow,
To thank all those who've trusted me to keep the books and treasury.
I'll speak for Don and Blake as well, who've served the board this four-year spell.
We've had a very spicy time, with issues that are hard to rhyme.

We've seen our peacock's fortunes go from third to someplace we don't know.
We've seen for years, our best advice slide down the drain like melting ice.
We've often heard, sometimes believed, that daylight soon would be perceived,
That with our faith and strong support, our ship would soon sail into port.

We've seen a score of prime-time shows that fail 'cause no one ever knows
Just when a fan can hope to see, the best we have on NBC,
A paradox that we've also known, for on the peacock's shaky throne
Has sat someone we've come to know as caring, working, on-the-go.

A man we truly call our friend, who's tried his level best to mend
A weakened network, poorly run; his job has surely been no fun.
We wish him well, for he deserves a straight pitch, no more off-beat curves.
Instead of brickbats he must duck, his tireless work deserves some luck.

We leave our board in damned good form, a chairman equal to the storm,
Successors whom you know as well will serve us all and work like hell.
Our cause we've pushed 'til voice was hoarse; our time on stage as run its course;
While other hands take up the slack, for now, we three will fade to black.

II

I want to say a word about our friend, Don Shaw.
We, from the mountain, who have known and worked with him for some thirty years, will long recall Don as the archetype of the best traits we associate with the term "Yankee."
Honorable—his word was better than bond;
Reliable—you could set your watch by the accuracy of his comings and goings;

Competent —his methodical, patient temperament always meant thorough care of the material in his charge;
Conservative and frugal— these concepts were his only standards of conduct;
Dry and seemingly humorless —a man of few unnecessary words. Were he to know that so many of us had come here today out of love and respect for him, his reply would be that familiar "Oh, No!"
But that is, indeed, why we are here assembled, for it is all too true in human affairs that we speak our best lines at the end.

III

On this occasion it's my task, to set a scene in which can bask,
In well-deserved and rightful pride, a man who's been our friend and guide.
A young broadcaster once was I, so long ago it makes me sigh;
And to his office I would go, when Harry Bannister said, "No!"

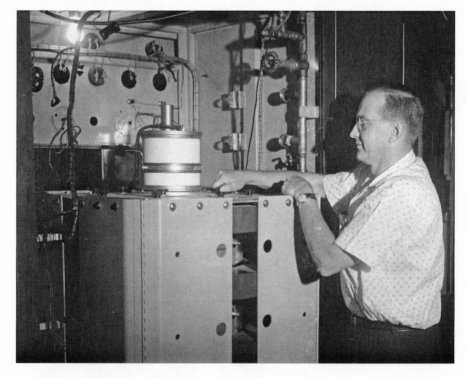

Assistant Chief Don Shaw "dresses" and adjusts a spare klystron final amplifier tube.

Which word, it seemed, was all he knew, each time I asked for my just due.
But Don would hold me with a smile, "Have patience, son; just wait a while."
And as I've waited these thirty years, increases went to all my peers.
Please, Don, before you fade to black, just open up that till a crack.

When TV began, that was the time, our NBC ran, with a chime;
And when the troops got in a jam, we simply called for Walter Damm.
Then he, in turn, would pound and shout, and summon up his mighty clout.
The network brass would cringe with fear; the Great God Damm, he had no peer.

But Harry begot Tom and Don, then wrote a book and said, "So long."
And Walter gave his big baton to Harris and said, "Carry on."
One night the General had a dream, and peacocks came to grace our screen.
The color went to South and North, but chimes no longer sounded forth.

Then Texas Jack gave way to Read, who called on Hod when he had need;
And on Floor Six at 30 Rock, revolving doors came into stock.
The "N" took over from the snake, and ratings sweeps were like a wake.
The peacock hid itself in shame, and no one knew just who to blame.

Through all the turmoil of this scene, one man alone stayed cool, serene.
With crises surging 'round him fast, so cool was he, they surged right past.
But we, who've been here for a while, recall for all those years his smile;
As loyally for NBC, he made us steadfast equally.

To keep this whole unruly mob in line has been his daily job.
A task I'd relish not one bit; It calls for tact and work and wit.
And now that things are looking up, we're finally losing this old pup,
This man who's known us and who's cared how well his chickens each have fared.

So, at this time of pride and joy, we speak with love of our old boy,
For through the joys — and often tears — he's known us lovingly for years.
Tonight we're gathered from afar, to point that he's ahead of par.
We toast his health, his wealth and life, and Isabelle, his lovely wife.

Don Mercer's been our friend — it's true — and to the peacock's every hue;
If faith and honor are the test, Don Mercer stands among the best.

IV

When God began the FCC, He must have planned on Robert Lee;
He must have known that in due course, this man would be a mighty force;
And if as chairman he would sit, someday he'd need that Irish wit.
So now, we're gathered from afar, to tell him that he's beaten par.

He has not always voted right, and once he even ducked a fight.
Yet countless stations have existence, solely due to his persistence.

WWLP's 25th birthday party in 1978; Bill, Sol Paul (*TV Age*), Kitty, Hon. Robert Emmet Lee.

For UHF his name once stood; for us he did 'most all he could;
But few of us today recall, how he gave hope and help to all.

I shall not dwell too much on that, though if I waxed on all I know
Perchance he still might throw the book, and surely I would get the hook.
So I'll content myself to state the facts that I can best relate;
For licensees are precious few, who've known and loved him as I do.

Rare too is the licensee, whose ticket from the FCC
Predates the time in '53, when I met Robert Emmet Lee.
So I'm among a smallish crowd, who have the right to speak aloud
And think of him among my peers, though I spot him several years.

He's recognized the world we're in, keeps few of us from every sin;
And no one serves the public who is off the air with payroll due.
Another truth he's also known: that not all wisdom is his own,
That often in some far-off spot, they may have learned an awful lot.

Indeed, he's often told his friends to thank the Lord and make amends,
That from our government we get, far less than all our tax would let.
Or putting it another way, be glad your money goes astray,
We surely would regret the day, that we were ruled for all we pay.

Commissioner Lee, our honored guest, is two cuts better than the rest
He's served the public trust with grace, while earning for himself a place
That no one else will ever find, deep in our common heart and mind.
He thus becomes a ruler rare, one that's open, fun and fair.

When once the EIA crowd tried to stem the flowing tuner tide,
I called them names, but softly he said "do not blame the MST
For they've as much at stake as you, in bringing all the service due
And soon you'll find both U and V have common cause in free TV."

"Indeed," said he, "the day will come, when they'll all say I'm not a bum;
And Putnam, you'll a mossback be, the day I leave the FCC."
I scoffed and thought he'd flipped his wig; a deal like that he'd never rig.
But, as I look upon this crowd, I recall he said it, right out loud.

And so we've gathered on this day, our thanks to give, our words to say,
That as from now, you fade to black, one thing for sure you'll never lack:
A host of friends who'll cherish you, your wit, your grace, your wisdom, too;
You give us love and joy and mirth, and serve both God and man on Earth.

In 1983, Bill delivered his final verse as one of the NBC-TV Affiliates; he had not meant it to be his last, but nevertheless it summed up a long relationship, and named a lot of names.

There are strange things done, when off their bun, by the folk at 30 Rock.
And without that nun it's a bit more fun, in the roost with our peacock.
Now, in order to report to you what's really in the cards,
One blissful day I snooped my way, just like the old time bards.
To write this ditty, in New York City, I had to show my feet,
To the shoeshine man, as he often can tell more than the elite.

Kitty and Bill, among the oak trees outside our third-floor office door —1983.

As we've all found, they shift their ground, depending on the rating;
What's good right now, may not somehow be always worth restating.
Though big shots mix around Floor Six, the same as in the past;
The working folk, this is no joke, have risen up the mast.
Some forty floors behind glass doors, they've gathered up the pieces;
Just name your care, all things are there, except for rate increases.

Mapes, Flynn and more, big shots galore; they all have corner suites.
There's eight at least, a fulsome feast of decorative treats.
But where I'm from all walls are plumb, we build a place foursquare.
And thus I fear that we may hear strange things from this new lair.
These seven years, with many tears, they've learned that down is up;
But now that they're smack out of square, they'll never fill our cup.

Marazzi's word is "We ain't third; Forget what Nielsen said,
From six to eight on at least one date, We broke out of the red."
But for us cats this race for rats, we're told has skies of blue;
And I think I've heard on recent word, that some of it is true.
So "Pier," said I, "Please do not lie; just tell it like it is
That Christmas tree, which was to be, From some forgotten whiz,

Unless I'm wrong, it's grown along, there in the great outdoors.
And when it's cut, I'll bet my nut, we'll have some two by fours."
Said he to me, "Rest comfortably. Bill Rubens has the scope
From eight to ten with ancient men, we now have learned to cope.
We've also learned what others spurned, that after paying taxes
Those old male goats still sow wild oats, and all of them have axes.

"And furthermore, a treat's in store. Among our biggest deals
It is a fact, we've a new contract, to show the rest of *Wheels*."
"But Pier," I cried, "You've often tried to score a ratings coup,
Yet our numbers squirm just like a worm; what can our salesmen do?"
"Have faith," said he, "In what you see; Iaricci sells it easy;
There is no need to feel you're treed, or even slightly queasy.

Art Watson's sports are of all sorts, each contract neat and tidy.
No over-run will spoil your fun; we still remember *Heidi*!"
"And that tree you sneer from yesteryear, I pray you'll not disdain;
It's freshly felled and firmly held, on board the *Supertrain*.
But place your bet that there's life yet, and much that's nice to learn,
Tell Chairman Fred he's still well fed; I move, sir, we adjourn."

Now when I came into this game, thirty years and more ago;
'Twas NBC that said to me, "Don't stand there in the snow.
Come join our show and help us grow; we'll promise you a ride."
The which I did, with a bump and a skid; it was a flowing tide.
I've not been cold; but I'm growing old, with some I do call "friend."
"And that," say I, with a tear in the eye, "is a lovely way to end."

Appendix A

[KBP] One of the more long-lasting projects that Bill Rasmussen brought to us was the idea of having me compose a cookbook. While editorially simple, for I had most of my recipes on 3 × 5 file cards, this turned out to be a much longer-lasting project than we originally intended. Then, when I became Mrs. Putnam and William and I were ensconced at the Lowell Observatory, we published a second edition (Appendix B), which not only featured me on the front cover, but had a second picture of me on the back — standing beside a huge marlin which Loreto McNaught/ Davis and I had managed to apprehend during a visit to Cabo San Lucas. At that time, Loreto's husband, Ian (Mac), was president of the World Federation of Alpine Societies (UIAA), of which my William was the North American delegate, later an honorary member, and the two of them spent hours on the granite sea cliffs near the area's famous "Arco," so we ladies took up sport-fishing.

The original cookbook project soon became much more than a cookbook. In addition to numerous recipes — some of which I still find sufficiently tasty that we decided to include a few of my favorites in this appendix — the original book also included unwarranted and uncomplimentary (so William claimed) references to the senior half of Springfield Television's management; pictures of me at numerous public functions; pictures of various other station personnel; and numerous plugs for my sponsors, a good many of whom have since gone out of business — obviously because they no longer had me to speak for their virtues.

Copies of this cookbook were sold, occasionally; but most were given away as sponsor displays in various supermarkets throughout the WWLP coverage area. Later, we even found one offered on eBay.

Caution — since moving to the high country of northern Arizona, I have had to adapt many of my recipes to accommodate the lower boiling temperature of 7,200 feet (2,200 meters) above sea level, as well as the delayed impact of baking powder at this elevation. But the following recipes are what I still use — precisely — when I'm cooking for my daughters nearer sea level during our visits back East.

Strawberry Pie

Ingredients:

1 quart of de-stemmed strawberries (check for signs of mold at the bottom of the container before buying);
¾ cup sugar;
½ cup water;
1½ tablespoons corn starch (mixed with 2 teaspoons of water to form a paste);
1 pre-baked pie shell.

Crush 1 cup of strawberries and bring to a boil with ½ cup of water. Cool, then line the pre-baked pie shell with whole strawberries. Add corn starch paste to crushed strawberries and continue cooking on low heat until the mixture is thick and shiny (a few drops of red coloring added here will make the result brighter looking). When the mixture is thick, pour over the pie shell and chill. Add whipped cream before serving to 6 or 8 persons.

Bill's late friend, Sam Goodhue, who lived by himself in a White Mountain farmhouse, used to take this recipe and mix in rhubarb (which he grew outside the old barn beside his house) for half the volume of strawberries, thereby making an equally tasty pie.

Lobster Thermidor
(adapted from the famous Highland Hotel formula)

Start with a boiled lobster weighing about 1½ pounds. Split the critter lengthwise and take out the meat, including that from the claws. (William, a genuine Yankee, says he likes the green liver and, in early summer, the red roe; so save them aside. But, of course, he can also distinguish the male lobsters from the hens before they are cooked and loves the small, sweet meat inside the 8 legs.)

Dice the lobster meat (toss the empty claws, but save the main body shell).

Other Ingredients:
5 medium fresh-peeled and sliced mushrooms;
1½ cups of half & half (the Highland used heavy cream);
2 ounces of dry sherry;
2 egg yolks;
1½ tablespoons of white flour;
¾ oz. butter;
pinch of salt;
paprika;
Parmesan cheese;
½ cup of cracker meal.

Melt the butter in a saucepan, add sliced mushrooms, then simmer for 1 minute; Mix flour to a smooth paste with butter and mushrooms; Preheat the cream (half & half) in a double boiler, then add to the flour mixture, stirring constantly until it begins to thicken; Place the lobster meat (along with the liver and roe) in and stir until it comes to a boil; Add egg yolks — beaten with sherry, paprika and salt.

Now, place the cooked ingredients inside the empty shell; Sprinkle the Parmesan and the cracker meal over the lobster mix; then place the reassembled critter on a flat pan, buttressed with some rock salt to prevent it from sliding around, and bake at 400 degrees Fahrenheit for 15 minutes.

Another recipe we came to like from the famous old Highland Hotel, which had been operated since 1915 by the managerial and culinary staff from the interned NordDeutscher Lloyd liner, *Kronprincessin Cecilie*, was one for a Chauvinette (William still orders one, every time we have dinner at Springfield's newer but equally noteworthy Student Prince [and Fort] German restaurant). The mix starts with three parts of Creme de Cocoa, four parts of Galliano and four of Grand Marnier; then this assemblage of liqueurs is thoroughly shaken with some crushed ice and vanilla ice cream, and served instead of a dessert in a mid-sized, short-stemmed wine glass.

Barbecue Sauce

Since living in Arizona — albeit the cactus-free, northern part, above the Mogollon Rim — I have watched my new friends (whose taste buds were obviously incinerated in their early youth) shake Tabasco sauce into a bowl of good New England–style clam chowder until it becomes entirely pink, and then douse the top with fresh ground pepper until the surface assumes a dark grey color — a culinary result which they routinely eat with gusto.

However, I have my own formula for a more civilized form of barbecue sauce (suitable for incurable gringos like William and me):

Ingredients:

1 teaspoon each of salt, chili powder, and celery seed;
¼ cup (or less) of dark brown sugar;
¼ cup plain cider vinegar (don't need fancy wine vinegar for this);
¼ cup Worcestershire sauce;
1 cup of tomato ketchup;
2 cups water;
a few drops of Tabasco.

Simmer the above mix for half an hour and then — if you're still able to smell — add a few dollops of minced (or grated) onion and garlic to the result.

Lasagna

Here in Flagstaff, I have learned that old-time Anglos in Arizona only eat beans and beef— the vegetables I find essential, as well as the meat from birds, fish or lesser four-legged critters, are for women, Eastern dudes, Mestizos and Orientals. But lasagna is different, and even members of the local sheriff's posse can often be teased into eating it. A main course for 8 goes as follows:

Ingredients:

1½ pounds of ground beef;
¼ cup chopped celery;
1 medium onion, chopped;
1 clove of garlic, minced;
2 tablespoons of lard, or drippings;
2 20 oz. cans of cooked tomatoes;
1 6 oz. can of tomato paste;
2 teaspoons salt;
¼ teaspoon cayenne pepper;
½ teaspoon oregano;
1 bay leaf;
1 8 oz. package of lasagna, or broad noodles;
2 cups ricotta, or cottage cheese;
1 lb. mozzarella cheese, sliced;
⅓ cup grated Parmesan cheese.

Heat the celery, onion and garlic in lard or drippings until tender; add ground beef and brown until crumbly but not hard. Pour off the drippings. Add tomatoes, paste, salt, pepper, oregano and that bay leaf. Cover and cook gently for 20 minutes; then remove the bay leaf.

Cook noodles in boiling, salted water until tender; then drain and arrange half of them in a greased 4-quart baking dish. Pour half the meat mixture over the noodles and cover with a layer of ricotta and mozzarella. Repeat with the remaining noodles, meat sauce and cheese. Sprinkle the surface with Parmesan and bake at a moderate temperature (350 degrees) for 30 minutes.

Stuffed Mushroom Caps

Of an evening, we often have a cocktail before dinner (William prefers a very wet and "dirty" Martini or a sweet Manhattan — while I prefer a chilled glass of *viognier* or *pino grigio*, of which latter William insists on buying only the products derived from, or grown in, the dolomitic soil of wineries in the Alto Adige (where he finished up his combat activities in World War II). On our more peaceful evenings, when we don't have company, I will often prepare the following canapé dish:

Ingredients:
8 medium-sized mushroom caps;
½ cup of cooked pork sausage meat;
2 tablespoons of Burgundy wine;
a generous dash of red pepper.

Scoop out the centers of the mushrooms and fill with the meat and wine mixture. Place under a broiler until the mushrooms are tender and the meat slightly browned. Be sure to have some liquid in the bottom of the pan, so the mushrooms will not adhere to it when cooking. Spike with extra-sized toothpicks to serve hot.

A No-Work Dinner

Sometimes I am required (by the local trustee I live with) to preside at an afternoon social function, and will have little time to prepare light dinner for six, so I often fall back on a "busy day" casserole, which is inexpensive and can be made ahead, as follows:

Ingredients:

1 pound of ground beef (I always ask my butcher for the low-fat kind);
1 cup of uncooked rice;
1 package of onion soup mix;
1 can of cream of mushroom soup;
1 cup of water.

Break up the ground beef with a spatula and combine it with the onion soup mix (it is not necessary to brown the meat first). Add the mushroom soup and water, tossing lightly to ensure that everything is thoroughly combined. Finally, add the rice and stir it thoroughly into the slurry. Place the result in the fridge until needed.

The casserole is now ready to make itself. Just pop it into an oven at 350 degrees for an hour. As a final touch, I will often remove the casserole dish and sprinkle it with some finely sliced onions and grated Parmesan cheese. Return the casserole to the oven until the cheese melts — and dinner is done.

Blueberry/Lime Jam

My children — as well as William — have told me it is obvious that when I am burned up (or bummed out) by some event (most often it's William's misbehavior) I will commence to make jam or jelly. William says this explains why I have so many jelly jars that a wide pantry shelf is devoted to them. He also growls about the alleged fact that when I am engaged in one of these enterprises, I take up the whole kitchen with the equipment and ingredients necessary for making a batch. However, I have yet to encounter the individual who fails to expropriate a jar or two of my jams when given the chance. Anyhow, my daughter, Erica, has come up with this recipe which yields five 12 oz. jars:

Ingredients:

4½ cups of blueberries;
1 tablespoon of grated lime peel;
⅓ cup of lime juice;
6½ cups of white sugar;
2 pouches (6 oz.) of liquid pectin.

Place the blueberries in a large saucepan, add the lime peel, lime juice and sugar; stir well and bring the mixture to a full, rolling boil, stirring constantly. Remove from heat and stir in the pectin.

Meantime, I have been boiling the jelly jars (and their lids) into which the jam is going to be poured, to be sure they are thoroughly clean and receptive.

Now, pour the cooling blueberry mixture into the hot jars that have been lined up on a large tray — leaving a space of ¼ inch unfilled at the top. Pour about ¼ inch of hot paraffin on top (to provide a tight seal). Apply their caps and relax while things cool down.

I generally affix dated labels while I remember what is in which.

Appendix B

[KBP] When my first cookbook, *At Home with Kitty*, was published, cholesterol was not a (dirty) household word, and every good hostess felt it her duty to serve lots of nourishing food with beautifully executed desserts, mainly chocolate, and go heavy on the whipped cream. Sauces and gravies were the order of the day and plenty of butter was an ingredient of importance in most dessert recipes. Barbecuing was the summer cuisine, at which potato salad with lots of eggs and mayonnaise was a sure winner.

As the American people — precious few of whom lead truly active lives, these days — became more aware of the consequences of heavy eating and started to opt for smaller portions and less fat, our cooking habits also changed. "Less Fat," "Lite," and "No sodium" began to appear on food labels and we started to cook differently. I have reflected some of these changes, partly due to the influence of Darlene Ryan and her husband, Peter Rosenthal, who helped me prepare the second edition, which they entitled *Cooking with Kitty, Today!*

Something else happened in the last few years — we began to be more concerned with presentation. We have been decorating the serving platters, adding grapes and pieces of cut fruit to give some color, and adding many varieties of nut to salads and even some main dishes.

In the last thirty years, more and more young mothers, like my daughter, Erica, have entered the regular workforce, often, like Erica, in inventive and executive capacities, and from a desire for independence, not mere survival. Therefore, unless they are abnormally adroit, they have less time to devote to home cooking, so America's food manufacturers and markets have responded and are replete with packaged main courses and even entire meals — and "take out" has become a household phrase. When I was pretty much forced into the workplace, back in 1951, mothers of that era felt guilty all the time we were away from our household duties and children, consequently we spent our limited time at home, trying our best to be like "stay-at-home" mothers, cooking large, nutritious meals every evening as well as on weekends.

As long as I still like to cook, though William complains about having to help clean up the kitchen unnecessarily often, I still look for new recipes. But even if I live to be over 200, I'll never be able to make routine use of them all. However, the first recipe I offer in this second appendix was derived from my mountaineering, woodsman, adventure-loving husband, who described it as "high class" and used the French term Roti de Bouc Montagnaise, which I think is a fancy French way of saying "roast mountain goat." Bill modestly — which for him is quite an effort — refuses to take sole credit for this recipe, giving some of that credit (read "blame") to another of his old mountaineering friends, the late Dr. Benjamin Greely Ferris, Jr. Here's the way William put it:

The most difficult part of this entire recipe lies in obtaining the necessary main viand. I have never seen "rack of goat" on sale in any butcher shop or run-of-the-mill supermarket. Thus, one must almost always go to the source for the basic ingredient.

I have generally found that source in the wilder mountains of British Columbia, but those willing to take a short-cut — and perhaps run the risk of lengthy imprisonment and/or a very stiff fine — can easily walk right up to quite a few mountain goats in the more protected areas of many national, or even city, parks. That choice is up to the preparer. In any case, my personal list of necessary implements for preparing this dish generally starts out with a .30-06 rifle.

After obtaining the necessary main ingredient, generally known in scientific circles as *Oreamnos montanus*, the next part of the process requires divesting the meat of its hide and hair. This is not an activity for the squeamish, or most city-bred folk, and requires the use of a sharp knife (perhaps an axe, too) along with a lot of patience. Before this part of the process is complete, the chef will have noticed and hopefully obtained four excellent racks of *oreamnos*, as well, perhaps, as a mountable trophy, the former of which can be skewered onto a spit (green wood or metal) for ease of positioning over an open flame. The length of time required for cooking varies inversely with the distance the spit is held (or positioned) from the flame. (Sometimes the cooking time has also to be related to the age of the *oreamnos*, in which cases Dr. Ferris suggests steaming the meat, prior to placing it on a spit.) But a low flame with ample hot coals is far preferable to a raging inferno. If the meat is rotated slowly, while being held at a distance of some 15 cm (6 inches) from the coals, cooking time can run from ten to fifteen minutes. Serve with a small, sharp knife.

One of the greater benefits of this delicacy is that it does not require extensive culinary devices or apparatus, such as are commonly found in most domestic environments. A wood fire on open ground will do quite nicely (but be sure to prepare the fire-site adequately to prevent it from spreading).

Much though I love my husband, for myself, I prefer what I call a:

Very Berry Summer Pudding

Ingredients:

2 cups blueberries;
⅔ cup sugar;
2 cups strawberries;
2 cups raspberries;
1 cup blackberries.

Buy (or bake) a cake of your choice (angel food, sponge, or one of your own) and slice thinly.

Heat blueberries with sugar to boiling, over medium heat, stirring often. Boil for 1 minute.

Stir in the remaining ingredients and continue cooking for another 2 minutes. Then let cool.

Line a baking dish with plastic wrap, allowing the ends of the wrap to hang well over the sides of the dish. Arrange slices of the cake in the dish, fitting them together. Layer in some of the berry mixture, then cover with more slices of cake, then berries. Be sure to end with a layer of cake on top.

Pull the plastic wrap over the final layer and weigh it down with heavy cans on top of dishes.

Refrigerate for 24 hours, until the pudding is firm on top and the cake slices are saturated with the berry juice.

Spoon into sherbet dishes (or glasses) and offer with some whipped cream or vanilla ice cream to serve a group of eight.

This recipe goes well, after — or perhaps in place of— a main entree of rack of goat.

A copy of the first edition of my cookbook found its way to a remote cabin in the mountains of British Columbia (not too far from Ed Wallis's gas station) and was ultimately returned to its author. On the originally blank back page was a penciled-in recipe signed: *"Good Luck! LaVerne."* It read:

Pico de Gallo Dip

Peel 2 avocados and chop them finely with 1 cup of onion. Add ½ teaspoon pepper and 1 tablespoon of concentrated lemon juice. Mix; then add 2 finely chopped chilis and 2 finely chopped tomatoes. Blend in 1½ teaspoons of salt, 1 tablespoon of cilantro (coriander) and 2 tablespoons of bottled Italian salad dressing. Serve with cocktails and corn chips, any afternoon, on a sun-lit deck in the alpine area of any mountain range.

Aunt Kim Potatoes

It's never too late to learn a new recipe, and I cheerfully admit that I stole the following idea from my daughter-in-law, Kimberly, but it's quite easy to prepare and all our grandchildren love it:

Figure on 3 or 4 small red potatoes per person dining and cut them in pieces that are not much larger than one cubic inch. Place on a shallow pan and sprinkle lightly with olive oil. (Kim sometimes sprinkles a packet of onion soup mix over the whole tray before baking, so as to enhance the flavor.) Bake at 350 degrees for thirty minutes.

Summer Garden Casserole

This is great served with barbecued steak. I got it from a self-styled "old cow-hand" in northern Arizona:

Ingredients:

3 cups yellow, crook-necked squash;
3 cups zucchini;
1 green bell pepper;
1 sliced onion;
2 cups of quartered Roma tomatoes;
2 cups of shredded cheddar cheese.

Cut up and sauté the squash, zucchini, pepper and onion; cover; continue on low heat until almost tender. Add the tomatoes and continue cooking until the desired tenderness is achieved. Sprinkle with the cheddar cheese. Cook until it is melted, then remove from heat. Serves eight.

Mushroom Lasagna

There are several variations on this formula, some of which can be read in the Barefoot Contessa's works, and others of which can be found referenced on Jack Clifford's *Food Channel*. I prefer, however, the variation which Darlene Ryan and her friend, Annie Bennett, have made for me. Since William likes this variation, I have been coerced into risking the charge of plagiarism, but suggest that the addition of spinach should be sufficient to keep the lawyers off my neck as well as to satisfy my need to provide at least one significant and traditional vegetable for every meal.

You'll need the following list of items to make a dish that serves eight hungry vegetarian people:

Olive oil and kosher salt;
¾ lb of dry lasagna noodles;
4 cups of whole milk;
1½ sticks of unsalted butter;
½ cup of all-purpose flour;
1 tsp freshly ground black pepper;
1 tsp ground nutmeg;
1½ lb portobello mushrooms;
1 cup freshly ground Parmesan cheese;
2 cups of freshly cooked spinach.

There are several ways to make the necessary white sauce — you can even buy some packets for this purpose in many stores. But, if you are a purist, do the following:

Heat the milk to a simmer and set aside. Then melt 1 stick of the butter in a low heated saucepan; slowly add in the flour, stirring constantly to prevent lumpy clots. Pour (William says "dump") the hot milk into the butter/flour mix and add the salt, pepper and nutmeg, stirring constantly with wooden spoon or a whisk. When it begins to thicken, set it all aside.

Separate the mushroom stems from the caps and set the stems aside (I like to chop them finely to cook separately and put in soup). Slice the mushroom caps into ¼-inch-thick pieces, then sauté them in a separate pan with 2 tablespoons each of the oil and butter, until the mushrooms begin to get tender and start to release some of their juices. You may have to do this in two separate batches. Meantime, you should have chopped up the spinach and boiled it a bit in lightly salted water, then strained out the excess water.

To assemble the lasagna, spread some of the white sauce on the bottom of a mid-sized, 2-inch-deep baking dish; arrange a layer of noodles, then spinach and more sauce, then ⅓ of the mushrooms and ½ cup of the Parmesan cheese. Do all this twice more, so you end up with three layers of these classy ingredients, with ½ cup of the Parmesan on top.

You can freeze this concoction for later use, or (for immediate consumption) bake it for 45 minutes at around 375 degrees. William says: "It's yummy."

Index

ABC network 181
Adams, D. 107ff., 110, 203
Adams, S. 197
AFTRA (union) 135
Agnew, Hon. S. 85
Allen, S. 134
antenna gain 18
Appalachian Mountain Club 15, 167
Artists Bluff 165
As Schools Match Wits 43ff.
Asnebumskit Hill 19, 186
Astronomy 194
AT&T 30
Aunt Kim Potatoes 227
AWRT 75, 165

Babe (elephant) 72
Back, F. 40
Bahakel, C.N. 140
Bal de Tete 50
Balaban, E. 109
barbecue sauce 219
Bartley, Hon. D.M. 156
Bartley, Hon. R.T. 201
Beach, W. 68
Beesemeyer, R. 185
Benny, J. 71
Berle, M. 69
Biersack, G. 185
The Big Picture 45
Blair, F. 114
blueberry/lime jam 222
Boilard, A. 131
Boland, Hon. E.P. 85, 158, 194
Boss, E.F., MD. 30
Boulware, L. 22
Boyer, A.J. 61
Boyle, Hon. J. 155
Bozo (guide) 96
Brady, J. 85
Bresnahan, P. 91

Bridges, L. 62
Brissette, P.A. 197
Broadcasting Hall of Fame 82
Broman, E. 78, 98, 149, 196
Broman, M. 78, 111, 195
Brooke, Hon. E. 85
Brown, B. 68, 135
Burch, Hon. D. 202
Burger, A.B. 109
Busch, Sgt. B. 46
Byrne, B. 111, 204

Cadwell, H. 61
Cannon Mountain 126
Cardigan Mountain 167
Carter, R. 59
Chase, S., Esq. 162
Chenevert, L. 51, 81
Chisman, T. 31
Cliff, Hon. E. (USFS) 142
color television 40ff.
Colton, T. v, 55, 86, 129
Conte, Hon. S.O. 85
Corio, A. 69
Coulters pine cones 141
Cowen, E. 144
Cox, Hon. K. 200
Craney, E.B. 119
Creep, Dr. 180

Daley, J.L.P. 184
Davis Amendment 161
Dawson, Hon. A.O. 42
Dayton (city) 178
Dean, P. 124
Deliso, J.J. 14, 88, 98, 103
Dempsey, Hon. J.N. 176
Dingell, Hon. J. 172
Discovery Communications 147
Dodge, J.B. 140
Doerfer, Hon. J. 161, 173

231

Doherty, P.T. 95, 110, 125
Donahue, R. 206
Douyard, D. 138
Drury, R. 135
Dumont, A.B. 104
Dunham, A.C., Esq. 6, 204
Dunham, J.B. 156

Eden, B. 59
Emerson, Hon. F. 18
Emerson, L.P.B., Esq. 153
English, J.W., Esq. 171

Faber, W. 204
Fairness Doctrine 2, 152, 199
Fashion Week 74
FCC: rulings 45; 6th report 16
Fergie, J.A. v, 30, 163, 171, 178, 189
Ferguson, J.H. v, 61, 83
Ferguson, R. 144
Ferris, B.G., Jr., MD 225
Ferriter, M., Esq. 91ff.
Fessenden, R.A. 4
Fiedler, A. 58
Filiault, R.L. v, 25, 28, 50, 64, 73, 143
Firestone, M.E., Esq. v, 148, 181, 189ff.
Fitzgerald, T.P. 14
Flynn, K.E. 178
Forbes & Wallace 3, 77, 134
Ford, Hon. F. 161
Ford, Hon. G. 146
4X150 (tubes) 22
Frost, R.L. 114ff.
Furcolo, C.L., MD 14

General Electric Co. 21ff.
Gerecht, M. 139
Ginsburg, C. 40
Gmoser, J.W. (Hans) 91, 99
goats 38
Golub, B. 181
Goodman, J. 107
Graves, E. 155
Greely, Gen. A.W. 4
Green, W. 80
Gunsmoke 76
Guzewicz, H. 27, 38
Guzewicz, W. 27, 38

Halas, G. 136
Half a Horse Award 140
Hamar, P. 208
Harris, J. 144, 176, 191
Harris, W. 135
Hatch, E. 137
Hays, Gen. G.P. 46

Hedin, A. 51, 92
Hemmerle, H.G. 127
Hennock, Hon. F.B. 199
Henry, Hon. E.W. 200
Hertz, H.R. & Waves 3
Highland Hotel 51
Hildreth, Hon. H. 124
Hill, Bennie 170, 192
Hinckley, Hon. R.H. 162
Hogan, Hon. T. 181
Hollingbery, G.P. 104, 123, 127
Hoover, J.E. 165
Huntley, C. 119
Hurley, Hon. M. 159
Hyde, Hon. R. 173, 200

Isles, D. 126

Jackson, R. 204ff.
Jacobs, R. v, 68, 136, 187
Jay, R. 32, 79
Jemima, Aunt 63, 73
Jenness, E., Esq. 177
Johnson, Hon. E. 32
Julian, B. 180

Karpowicz, R. 204
Kauffman, A.J. 9, 177
Keefe, H. v, 90
Kelly, J., Esq. 182
Kennedy, E.M. v, 12, 94, 125
Kennedy, Hon. J.F. 9, 47, 137
Kennedy, R. 58
Kenny, P. 111, 144
King, R.T., Esq. 13
Kittyhawk Television 180
Klein, B. 97
Knode, T.E. 186
Koop, C.E., MD 126
Koop, D. 126
Kronprinzessin Cecilie 53
Krueger, R. 204
KSTU (TV) 192

Lambert, E. 74
Langevin, R. 71, 139
Lasagna 220
Latham, W.H. 55
Lawrence, Rt. Rev. W.A. 163
Leahy, E. 148
Lee, Hon. R.E. 2, 29, 41, 89, 161, 164,
    168, 199, 211
Leovinger, Hon. L. 201
Lescoulie, J. 118
Liberace 69
Lin Broadcasting Co. 1

lobster thermidor 218
Low, H. 45
Lowell, A. 115, 203
Lowell, P. & Observatory 1

Madsen, A. 191
Magnusson, Hon. E. 172
Maguire, Rev. J. 90
Malaine, J. 91
malamutes 149
March of Dimes 117
Marconi, M.G. 4
Marek, L. v, 48, 53, 133, 138
Marek, M. 48, 51, 91
Mark Hopkins Hotel 109
Mass Mutual Life Insurance Co. 180
Massasoit, chief 15
Maxwell, J.C. 4
McCarthy, J.P., Esq. 6
McConnaughey, Hon. G. 161, 172, 202
McCormick, Hon. J.W. 108
McCormick, M. 204
McGee, M. v, 50
McKenna & Wilkinson 153, 162
McMahon, Jas. 20
McMahon, Jos. 182
McQuade, A.P. (Bus) 103
Mercer, D. 186, 210
Mercier, R. 27, 37
Metacomet, Chief & Trail 15
Meyer, A.C. 176
Minow, Hon. N.N. 9, 169, 175, 199
Mitchell, G.J. v, 53, 145, 178
Moeller, D. 204
Morrison, P. 68
mountain rescue 125
Mulroney, M. 121
mushroom caps 221
mushroom lasagna 228

NABET (Local 13) 49
Nail, D.B. (Tack) 7, 144, 168
National Association of Broadcasters 144, 146, 168ff.
National Telefilm Association 41
NBC-TV 105; preemptions of 43
Newhouse, S.I. 159
Newman, E. 118
Nizer, L., Esq. 42

Oakley, J. 14
Oaks Hotel 62
O'Connor, Hon. T.P. 157
Oktoberfest 97
O'Neill, Hon. T.P. 111
Overmyer, D.H. 188ff.

Pall Mall cigarettes 125
Pastore, Hon. J.O. 172
Patti, C. 180
Paul, Sol 212
Le Pavillion 109
Paxton, F. 207
Payne, A. 204
peninsula *see* WVEC
Pepin, W. 125, 192
Peter, Paul & Mary 69
Petermann, J. 98
Peters, N. 136
Petersham (town) 42, 87
Pfeiffer, J.C. 111
Philip, King *see* Metacomet
pico de gallo (dip) 227
Pluto (planet) 2
Pratt, F. 30
Presti, B. 41
Provin Mountain 15, 128, 129
Putnam, C.J. (Mrs. R.L.) 112
Putnam, E. 11
Putnam, G. 10
Putnam, M.C.J. 194
Putnam, Gen R. 89
Putnam, Hon. R.L. 11, 84, 87, 185
Putnam, R.L., Jr. 38
Putnam, W.L., III 12
Putnam W.L., IV 119, 196

Quello, Hon. J.H. 200
Quill, J. 12, 131

Rabbi Ben Ezra 113
Rassmussen, W. 12, 100, 151, 217
Ray, M. 69
Red Sox 44
remote telecasts 50
Rennison, P. 24
Rice, Rev. F. 163
Richmond, L. 23
Ring, M.S. 39, 193
Rittenhouse, P. 83, 105, 134
Robator, H. v, 12
Romper Room 103
Rooney, M. 68
Roslow, Dr. S. 102
Roti de Bouc Montagnaise 225
Rusch, S. 118
Ryan, Hon, C.V., Jr. 158
Ryan, D. 228

St. Lawrence Seaway 120
St. Patrick's Day Parade 89
Samble, R. 61
Sanford, Hon T. 186

Sarnoff, Gen. D. 108
Sarnoff, R. 108
Sawyer, W.A. (Buzz) v, 181
Scheftel, H. (Buzzie) 108
Scibelli, Hon. A. 155
Scott, J.Y. 14
Service, R.W. 149
Severinson, "Doc" 134
Shaw, D.C. v, 37, 209
Shepardson, P. 44
Silver, K. v, 12, 86
Silverman, F. 111, 207
Sinclair Broadcasting 1
Sisitsky, Hon. A. 155
6AF4 (tubes) 21, 36
skiing 66
Slater, M. 54
Small, W. 144
Smith, K. 61
snowball fight 133
Solberg, K. 104
Speckels, F. 74
Storrowton music tent 68
Stough, R.M. 171
Streibert, T.P. (Sam) 126
Streisand, B. 76
Sugg, "Buddy" 109
Sullivan, D. 80
Sullivan, Chief F. 92
Sullivan, T.G. 180
Sullivan, Hon. W. 86
Swayze, J.C. 135

Taischoff, S. 120
Tarzian, S. 41
TASO 172
Tavern Club 123
Television channel allocations 6
Television Information Office 146
10th Mountain Division 46
Thanksgiving program 67
Theft (of props) 150
Thomas, H. 171
Thompson, T. 51
Tindal, A.C. 10, 102
Tinker, G. 111
Tirpitz, Adm. A. von 3
Tonight 134
Townsend, G.R. v, 24ff., 32, 36ff., 131
Translators (TV) 31
Travelers Insurance Co 176
Traviesas, H. 114
Triangle Publications 161
Turet, L. 171

TV Pulse 102

Ulm, Chief R. 154
Uranus (planet) 2

Vadnais, G. 14
Vadnais, H.J (Bob) v, 32, 34, 91
Van, R. 68
Vanderploeg, E. 124
Very Berry Summer Pudding 226
videotape machines 33, 40

Waite, K.M. v
Wallace, D., Esq. 154
Wallace, L.R. 125
Wallerstein, Prof. G. 194
Wallis, E. 94
Washburn, Hon. A.M. 200
Waxman, Hon. H. 172
Waybest turkeys 67
Wayside Inn 80
WBZ-TV 135
WCAX-TV 117
WCSH-TV 44
Weicker, Hon. L. 85
West, Mae 106
Western Mass Electric Co. 61
Wheeler, Hon. B.K. 119
White House Coffee 64
WHYN-TV 37
Wide, Wide World 113
Wise, H. 127
WKEF (WIFE-TV) 178
WMECo Hilites 62, 102
WNHC-TV 18, 161
Woolsey, Hon, J.M. 42
Wright, Hon J.C. 182ff.
WRLP (TV) 28, 79, 131
WSPR 13
WTAG 20
WVEC (TV) 31
WWLP: expansion of 130; swimming
    pool 143; water supply 133
WWOR (TV) (WJZB) 19ff.

Yager, J. 204
Young, G. 60

Zeldin, A. 192
Zeller, M. 95
Zenger, P. 156
zoom lenses 40, 51